RALLY

Communal Prayers
for Lovers of
Jesus and Justice

EDITED AND COMPILED BY

BRITNEY WINN LEE

FRESH AIR BOOKS®

Nashville

Cover design: Amanda Hudson | Faceout Studio
Cover imagery: Shutterstock
Interior design and typesetting: PerfecType | Nashville, TN

Print ISBN: 978-1-935205-31-9 | Mobi ISBN: 978-1-935205-32-6 | Epub ISBN: 978-1-935205-33-3

Printed in the United States of America

This book is dedicated to the communities who have made our love bigger.

And to my mom and dad for everything.

CONTENTS

CONTENTS

CONTENTS

CONTENTS

ACKNOWLEDGMENTS

Contributors: This book is yours. It is an understatement to say that it wouldn't have happened without you and the lives you lead that inform your prayers. Andrew, Bruce, Erin, Lydia, Kaitlin, Brandan, Angela, Diana, Dee Dee, Brendan, Iyabo, Tamara, Sandra, Osheta, Aundi, Elaina, Lindsy, Shannon, Elrena, Kenji, Josina, Stephanie, Cory, Rachel, Onleilove, Delonte, Jonathan, Tony, Sharifa, Michael, Kayla, Juan, Chris, Nikki, D. L., AnaYelsi, Cat, Jeannie, Dana, Gary, Zhailon, Michelle, Patrice, Rose, Tanya, Austen, and Breanna: I'm incredibly grateful for who you are, the work that you do, and the hope in which you rest. As a white, middle-class, millennial, Protestant woman whose privilege is not (always) lost on me, I am aware that it is my honor to be here with you, learning and working toward another world. Thank you for letting me come alongside.

To the decision-making crew at The Louisville Institute, who gifted this project with the financial resources it needed to take shape by way of the Pastoral Project Grant, thank you. Your support was a catalyst, and I find hope in that there are organizations in our world investing time and funding into changing the church. And to my small group of grant-recipient peers who first workshopped this book's beginning, I'll forever be grateful that you asked the hard questions.

Jonathan Wilson-Hartgrove offered a generous ear and his network, as he often has in my life of writing. Thank you, friend, for your guidance, your letter of recommendation, your willingness to put my hand in the hand of people like Elaina Ramsey, who led me to more and more possible contributors. Elaina, my sister, you are the real MVP of this work. Your persistent cheerleading, your tender and fierce heart, your beating of the bushes for those whose stories should be represented on these pages, your encouragement to follow that flickering light of litanies—all priceless gifts. Same cloth, you and I. Thank you.

To Don Golden, Shane Claiborne, and the rest of Red Letter Christians for connecting me to people who could connect me to people whose palms are on the plows of Good News (and who could write about it), I am grateful. Thank you, Fresh Air Books, for believing in a collection of needed prayers and for not censoring the content of and for the marginalized. To the lovely and gifted writers of the Redbud Writers Guild and to my Voxing pals

(Danielle, Josina, and Breanna), your support and feedback in grief, celebration, and roadblocks have meant the world to me.

Luke and Bridger, you make me want the world to be what these prayers suggest that it could and should be.

And to the Black and Brown communities, indigenous neighbors, people of color, disabled individuals, women and girls, LGBTQIA+ folx, migrant and refugee siblings, incarcerated image-bearers, people with mental illnesses, those living in poverty, repentant souls who wish to do better, homesick rejects, radicals, and ragamuffins: The world needs you. The world needs you to illuminate Jesus, to be a reminder of the importance of interdependence, and to show the way of freedom in surrendering power and false security in exchange for community and an edifying existence for all. Lead on, dear teachers. And thank you.

FOREWORD

This is not your grandmother's prayer book. Or if it is, I would really like to meet your grandmother.

Some of you considering this book may be new to prayer and not know where to start. Some of you may be seasoned churchgoers and still not know where to start when it comes to authentic prayer. Whoever you are, I'm so glad you have this book. This is one of those books you don't just read through; you savor it. You carry it with you. This is a prayer book for a revolution—a revolution of love and compassion and justice.

The following pages contain prayers of joy and prayers of lament, prayers for folks who have great faith and prayers for folks who would like to have more. Here you will find prayers not only for the victims of violence but also for the perpetrators of violence. You'll find reminders that God's love can heal the oppressed and the oppressors, and if we look closely in the mirror, we will see both within ourselves *as well as* the image of God.

You will find prayers that train you in the works of mercy and the holy habits of Christian discipleship—welcoming the immigrant and stranger, caring for the earth, simplifying your life. You will find prayers that purge you of the counterfeit religion posing as Christianity but looking nothing like Christ, prayers to help you exorcise the demons of white supremacy, power, violence, racism, and materialism. As I read *Rally*, I was reminded of the apostle Paul who spoke about putting on the "full armor of God" (Eph. 6:11, NIV)—and this is a way to "arm" yourself as a person of peace, living out the way of Jesus in a world so full of violence and hatred.

The introductions that lead into the prayers by so many friends I love and adore, written with such eloquence and grit, ground the words of their prayers in the world in which we live. Their words remind me of how Karl Barth urged us to preach with the Bible in one hand and the newspaper in the other. Otherwise, our faith becomes a ticket into heaven and a license to ignore the world, making it more about escaping the world than engaging in it. As it is often said, "Many Christians end up being so heavenly minded that they are not much earthly good." But for Britney and the contributors here, prayer is not only about going to heaven when we die but also about bringing heaven to earth while we live.

If we aren't careful, prayer can become a way of escaping and hiding from any responsibility that love might require of us. Sometimes when people say, "I'll pray for you," we know they don't plan to do anything else to help—like politicians who offer thoughts and prayers after yet another mass shooting. But authentic prayer leads us to act. It bears fruit in concrete action. We get off our knees and do something about injustice. We hear someone pray for a neighbor who needs a wheelchair ramp, and we leave the church service ready to organize some carpenters to build that ramp. When we ask God to move a mountain, God may give us a shovel. We become the answer for what we're asking. We realize that prayer is not just about us trying to get God to take action but about God trying to get us to take action. This book is about prayer, and it is about taking action.

The word *litany* used throughout the book may be new to some. Litanies are public prayers that invite active participation—not just something we listen to someone else pray and then say *Amen*. Litanies invite us to move together, in a call-and-response sort of way, kind of like dancing with one another. And because litanies require a call and a response, they remind us that they ought to be used in public. God's good news is not just meant to be "applied" in the world but demonstrated, proclaimed, and performed like a symphony, a ballet, a step-team routine, or a three-ring circus.

For many of the prophets of old, prayer was a form of public lament and protest, a way of awakening people to injustice and stirring people's hearts to take action. Sometimes we like to say in my community, "We are not just protesting; we are *protestifying*." We are not just naming what is wrong but proclaiming what it would look like to make it right again. That's what these prayers did for me. I know they will do the same for you.

Many years ago, I had a friend confess to me, "I feel pretty lonely. I find myself among inactive believers and unbelieving activists." He went on to share how deeply he longed for a community that embraced both prayer and action. As you pray these prayers, in private and in public, know you are not alone. You are praying with a cloud of witnesses around the world and across the centuries.

I am grateful for Britney Winn Lee and all the authors of these prayers. This book is a gift to the church and to the world. Jesus desires that we would be one as God is one. As we put our voices together, as we pray these prayers in harmony, and as we take action to put flesh onto them, may we be one as God is one. Amen.

—Shane Claiborne

INTRODUCTION

In front of a one-hundred-and-twenty-year-old chapel, where I sometimes offer liturgical services on topics of justice and faith, in Shreveport, Louisiana, well-manicured flower beds line a concrete path. I have thought a lot about that concrete path over the last couple of years and the land on which it rests semi-permanently. For whom has that path provided a warm invitation—the privileged or the marginalized, the rich or the poor? For whom has it offered a means of heartbreaking exit—how many Black and Brown persons have felt unseen, how many LGBTQIA+ persons have felt unwelcome? Who first lived on the path's land when the city was but woods, when indigenous families stewarded these acres and called them home? Who was terrorized on this plot when the river lands were fields—when this parish was given the name "Bloody Caddo" due to the post-Civil-War lynchings of Black people that took place here? Who walked this path while fighting for a new reality—who marched for civil rights, for the rights of women, for gun control, and for same-sex marriage? And who didn't?

The work for this book began during a time of great anxiety in this country and in the church. And in the years since, I've seen Black and Brown bodies that were disturbingly susceptible to police brutality, a migrant caravan marching toward a militarized "welcome," children held in cages and separated from their parents seeking safety, politicians whose rise to office made women feel less safe to exist, tiki torches of white supremacists haunting the night, violence begetting violence ignored or justified by Christians. These have been anxious days.

But in those same years, I've heard raised voices ready to fight for justice. I've seen art so evocative and important that I could not look away. I've heard howling songs, read hopeful scripture interpretations, and partaken in creative organizing. The old saw visions, and the young dreamed dreams. The determined sought to see God in the *other*, and the resolved sowed love in a hurting world. "Everybody was a little bit scared or angry," I imagine us saying about these years, "but we never forgot how to sing."

As I approached that old chapel on my way to work one morning some time ago, I felt heavy and defeated with the news of Earth's deteriorating climate and America's divided citizens. Additionally, what would later be known simply as "Charlottesville" had taken place the day before. I had been at my parents' house in Louisiana, fifteen hours away from the city in Virginia where protesters and counter-protesters had gathered. Like much of the United States, I followed a steady stream of social media updates covering the event's rising tensions. With my phone on the bathroom counter, I leaned over, head in hands, watching the screen as faith leaders gathered to sing down the ultra-nationalist attendees of the largest white supremacist event in recent history.

That afternoon, Heather Heyer was killed by a car intentionally rammed into a crowd of anti-racist demonstrators. As her name joined the ever-growing list of those lost on the battlegrounds of injustice—alongside Sandra Bland, Trayvon Martin, Philando Castile, Felipe Gómez Alonzo, Kendrick Castillo, Alton Sterling, Michael Brown (the list, devastatingly long)—I grew more afraid of being alive in this place at this time. I watched online and over texts as friends and faith leaders wondered aloud, "What will we say when we gather with our communities now?" The night was bleak and isolating.

But the morning brought with it small, stubborn reminders of life. In the sidewalk leading to the chapel, as I approached my work with a two-ton heart, I saw them: a row of three-inch-high purple blooms, bursting through the powerful and imposing concrete, frail but vibrant. *They're protesting*, I thought. *Life will not be held down forever.* Those plants offered the truth that I needed when I didn't know what to pray. Over the next few hours, I wrote a liturgical litany titled "Sound the Alarm," which is the first litany in this book. That piece led to a journey of rallying diverse and informed voices in an effort to create a collection of communal prayers that might further provide hope to those who could use a bit more.

The Greek word *leitourgia*, from which we get our word *liturgy*, is commonly translated as "the work of the people." In researching for this book, one of my favorite understandings of liturgy that I found was "a gift . . . for the relief of the needy."[1] And we all have needs, don't we? If our times have told us anything, it is this. We are a people who need one another, living in a world that needs renewal. This book is intended, in part, to be a gift for the relief of the needy, but it is also the protest of a communal voice that says to the abuse of power and the threat of death, *Life will break through—eventually. And every single time.*

Lamentations for injustices and declarations for a world restored, written by and for the people of God, are no more new than the sicknesses that necessitate them. We hear the same song in Amos and the Psalms, in Isaiah and Mary's Magnificat, in the cotton fields of a bloody South and the marches of the Civil Rights Movement and the new Poor People's Campaign. Prophetic artists and writers, grieving preachers, raging mamas, and fiery youths have things to say and things to make. We cannot offer one another enough resources right now for hope, connection, and reminders of the *imago dei* in our enemies and our oppressed neighbors. We cannot *not* be the shoots of life pushing through the cracks, the words for those who ache when they don't know what to pray. For these reasons, nearly fifty truly remarkable people have worked to create this collection of prayers—prayers that offer words of repentance and hope that can be said together as we gather and grieve, meditate and organize for such a time as this.

When I was younger, I believed written prayers tucked away in the pages of dusty hymnals to be stagnant, crafted by dead men with dead ideas. But when I became a part of an intentional community in my twenties that prayed each morning from *Common Prayer: A Liturgy for Ordinary Radicals* and shared the joys and losses of everyday life, liturgy became the thread in my soul that stitched me to a place and its people. When our community closed its doors a few years ago, the collective reading of the prayers was what I missed most. I miss it still.

Litanies offer a radical welcome to people in that they remove intimidation participants may feel in entering into communal prayer. Litanies say, *We are here, and the grace is that we can connect without the pressure to conjure, perform, or be anything other than what we are.* Litanies are a rhythmic dance laced with the lamentations and joy of old spirituals, a sacred inhale and exhale for when we find ourselves asking, *What will we say when we gather?* Litanies are about the collective breath, intended to center our action with mindfulness and togetherness, to be a resource for wordless people, to be a way for the Spirit to intercede, "[helping] us in our weakness" when we "do not know how to pray" (Rom. 8:26). I hope this book can be the catalyst for drawing near to one another so that we can remind ourselves and others that we are wildly loved, that we have been invited to love God with our whole beings and to love our neighbors as if they *were* our whole beings.

For those who are new to using call-and-response prayers, I should mention that this book was designed to be read in a communal context, typically with one voice calling (indicated by regular font) and the community responding (indicated by **bold font**). Some of the litanies are written as lamentations from the marginalized, while others are confessions from the privileged. I ask that anyone who reads or uses these litanies to respect and honor each litany's writer and their context. Not all prayers in this book are intended for all people, though each one can teach us something about our faith and our neighbors. May we consider who we ask to lead these litanies in our churches, faith communities, and gatherings. Is there an individual whose life and history makes them a better fit for leading the exchange? And may we consider where these prayers are leading us, as we hear our own experiences voiced or as we gain insight into others' experiences. Toward what research, action, and stories are the prayers directing us so that we may become the answers to our own prayers? How can we partner with others—perhaps even with a contributor in this book—to further our own contemplation and action?

This collection is not exhaustive. To those who do not see themselves and their grief in these pages, I apologize. I believe that we all are important and loved; I believe there is room for everyone in these spaces. May we keep writing and reading prayers until all God's people feel safe, seen, and heard.

Winter and weed-eaters and chemicals will come again. Those small, audacious purple flowers will be ushered back beneath the soil by powers that *seem* final and in control. But resurrection people know better. There is life coursing underneath the concrete that has always been there, that will always be there. And until the day when all that God first intended is all that there is, we will continue to point one another toward the cracks in a backward kingdom. Where the last are first. And the weak are strong. And the tiniest, persistent prayers and petals can break open an empire and turn it back toward beauty and full life for the whole world.

Keep gathering.

Keep creating.

Keep breathing.

Keep going.

Until we all are there,

Britney

Sound the Alarm: A Call to Draw Near During Troubling Times

Britney Winn Lee

In the evenings, when my feet are sore from the day's work and the clothes from Sunday's unfinished chores are souring in the washing machine, I turn off the dreadful news so that I might stir the mac and cheese, chase my son's dump truck, and avoid the worries of the world. Folks are tired, of this I'm certain.

As my son and I gallop down our hall, I think about my Twitter feed and the weight that I've absorbed just from reading short commentaries on current events and the festering wounds of US history. *I've got to stop following so many melancholic activists*, I think to myself, just seconds before remembering that they're the ones who are teaching me how not to look away. It's so important not to look away right now.

But people are weary and nervous. Folks are tired of riding the yo-yos of policy scares and rumors of war, tired of explaining why they matter, tired of loose lips and hateful tones and violent threats, tired of divisions and extremes. They're tired of watching humans be treated as less than human, tired of wondering if the church is going to make it, if our country's going to make it. Tired of trying to figure out what power and purpose and time they actually have to do anything. Tired of bad news. Desperate for good.

In response to this exhaustion, I wrote a litany for the fighters of the good fight who feel constantly bombarded with the waves of a suffering world. It is for anyone who may need the jolt of a communal reminder that we're not yet done here—that God's not yet done here. I wrote it for the foolishly hopeful, the irrationally resolved, those who woke up today—despite it all—ready to look for the overlooked and love them with all they've got. Those who, as Dorothy Day described, embraced the merciful morning with a willingness to cast their pebble into the pond. So "let us consider how to provoke one another to love and good deeds, not neglecting to meet together, as is the habit of some, but encouraging one another, and all the more as [we] see the Day approaching" (Heb. 10:24-25).

ONE: Calling all those partaking in a resurrected life,
Who have known a death that did not kill them.
ALL: Come those with very little left to lose
And those holding most things loosely but love.
We need you.

ONE: Come all who are almost indifferent and undone,
Who are wielding disappointment as vigor.
ALL: Come those who fell asleep in the soul's dark night
But have awakened with a heart full of hope.
We need you.

ONE: Come with your words—old, eaten, and new.
Come, though uncertain about where it's all headed.
ALL: Come with your aching need to be heard
And you who are new to the listening.
We need you.

ONE: Come resolved to creatively find third ways.
Come committed to not rushing out of tension.
ALL: Come with eyes unwilling to overlook injustice
And a heart unwilling to forgo celebration.
We need you.

ONE: Come ragamuffin, radical, rebel, repressed.
Come you who were wrong and willing to say it.
ALL: Come refusing to deny the stories of your people.
Come with the assurance of God's grace as your guide.
We need you.

ONE: Come marchers, intercessors, artists, and prophets.
Come newcomers and those who have tried, tried again.
ALL: Get close, get close, get closer now.
Draw near, ask questions, sing songs, take steps.
We need you together.

ONE: And together, we'll be patient and mercifully kind—
Not envying, boasting, prideful, or rude.
ALL: Not selfish, short-fused, score-keeping, or spiteful
But rejoicing in the goodness of what's to be shared.
We need you. We need you together.

ONE: Because together the movement keeps going.
Sound the alarm because love cannot fail.
**ALL: Come resisters, revolutionaries, the meek who inherit the earth.
There will indeed be a story to tell.**

ONE: And it is this: When the Light was threatened
All God's people said, "Let's go."
ALL: Let's go.

One Small Step: A Litany for Not Knowing Where to Start Regarding Issues of Justice

Andrew Wilkes

God is able to do exceedingly and abundantly more than we can ask for, think about, or imagine. When we recognize injustice, what we can ask for, think about, or imagine may seem like an insufficient response to the injuries affecting us. Feeling unequal to the task, we may avoid doing anything. Our individual responses—or even our institutional ones—in fact may be insufficient. Those possibilities notwithstanding, there is another, deeper truth: God uses seemingly insufficient things to effect justice, to bring about freedom.

We remember the slingshot defeating the giant, widows wearing down unjust judges, exiled people rebuilding broken walls, as we ask, "Faithful God, transcend our imaginations, interweave our labor with other communities, and cause the work of our hands, be they few or many, to accelerate the end of patriarchy, racialized capitalism, and inhumane religion."

In the name of Jesus our Liberator and life-renewing Savior, may we who yearn to interrupt injustice start where we are, use what we have, do what we can. If we begin the work, God will undergird it, ushering us and all of creation toward becoming the Beloved Community.

ONE: We affirm that liberation is the divine intent for all human beings, everywhere, in every age, especially for those who are oppressed, minoritized, and exploited.

ALL: Christ, set us free to experience freedom, justice, and peace.

ONE: We commit to upending injustice, working alongside those who are directly impacted.

ALL: Generous God, supply us with the courage to realize liberation by interrupting injustice.

ONE: We seek justice with discernment, rejecting the false ideal of having to know everything before starting anything.

ALL: All-wise God, help us distinguish between essential facts and non-essential perspectives so that we can take informed action for justice.

ONE: One small step to undo oppression is greater than an ambitious, undone deed.

ALL: Give us the strength to begin the work and the stamina to complete it.

ONE: Where do we begin to fight for liberation and justice?

ALL: Everywhere—in our homes and hearts, our schools and streets, our workplaces and public spaces, our churches and communities.

ONE: "For the weapons of our warfare are not merely human, but they have divine power to destroy strongholds."*

ALL: As disciples of Christ, we undertake the Spirit-filled work of pulling down the strongholds of institutional sin: structural racism, gender-based violence, and economic injustice.

ONE: "There is no longer Jew or Greek, there is no longer slave or free, there is no longer male and female; for all of you are one in Christ Jesus."**

ALL: In church and society, we pledge to dismantle hierarchies based on gender, disparities determined by race, and oppression in all its forms.

ONE: With Spirit-led determination and righteous resolve to be living liturgies, we affirm these words together:

ALL: We will not rest until all are free, all are whole, and all are home.

*2 Corinthians 10:4
**Galatians 3:28

A Prayer for Perpetrators

Michelle Thorne Mejia

When Jarrod Ramos opened fire at the *Capital Gazette* in Annapolis, Maryland, on June 28, 2018, the gun violence epidemic touched the town where I serve as pastor. Five people were killed that day. Five people never came home to their loved ones. This has become an all too familiar story throughout our nation.

In a vigil that brought together several United Methodist churches a few days after the shooting, I was asked to offer a prayer for the perpetrator of violence. The very human side of me immediately thought, *Everyone will be really upset that I am praying for him.* It's one thing to pray for the perpetrator when I'm not the one affected, but many of my parishioners knew the victims. This was personal.

Just as quickly as that thought entered my mind, Jesus' words began to echo in my heart: "Love your enemies and pray for those who persecute you" (Matt. 5:44). *How do I pray for those who seek to harm others?* I wondered. But I knew what I had to do. The following is the prayer that worked on my heart, allowing it to break open as I listened to the Spirit's words. How will we stop the cycle of violence if we can't learn to offer prayers for those who perpetrate it? This prayer is my attempt at learning to pray for those for whom I do not want to pray.

ONE: Beloved siblings, Jesus tells his followers, "Love your enemies and pray for those who persecute you."* In that spirit, let us now pray for the perpetrators of violence, including Jarrod Ramos, who took the lives of five individuals in his targeted attack at the *Capital Gazette* (or insert name of perpetrator and act of violence):

God over Golgotha, the place where Jesus died, when senseless acts of violence occur, we admit that praying for those who seek to harm, who aim to kill others, who take away the gift of life that you give is incredibly difficult.

ALL: It goes against everything that we think and feel and want in this moment.

ONE: But we remember that Jesus, in the place of Golgotha, even on the cross, spent one of his precious dying breaths speaking words of loving-kindness over those who crucified him.

ALL: **"Father, forgive them; for they do not know what they are doing."** **

ONE: So Jesus lived and died, staying true to what he asks of others.

ALL: **"Love your enemies and pray for those who persecute you."**

ONE: For those who harm others and who seek to do harm in this world, we pray, O God.
We remember them and all who love them.
We remember that their lives too are devastated and their hopes dashed.
We know that the pain from each act of violence, like the ripples of a stone cast in a pond, travel in many different directions.
Those who perpetrate violence become casualties of their own anger, their own hatred, their own bitterness, their own deep woundedness.
They too are in need of your grace, your love, and your healing light.

ALL: **They know not what they do.**

ONE: Help them see what they do.
Help them recognize the ripples of suffering and pain that have been caused by the stones they threw, by the guns they shot, by their own actions.
Not only do they not know what they do, but also they do not know what they need.

ALL: **So we pray with Jesus, "Father, forgive them."**

ONE: May that forgiveness begin to disarm their anger and hatred, dismantle their bitterness, and demolish their desire to harm.
May that forgiveness be a healing balm that begins to mend and transform the broken places and pain in their own lives.
Holy Spirit, who filled Jesus even on the cross at Golgotha, keep us from casting our own stones of anger, hatred, bitterness, and retaliation.

ALL: **The darkness cannot compare to the power of the light.**

ONE: May we be your light.
May we be catchers of stones and not casters of stones.
May we learn to love and forgive the way that you have and do.
May our work for justice include loving our enemies and praying for those who would persecute or harm us.

May our presence bring healing to this world, in the name of Jesus the Christ.
ALL: May it be so. Amen.

*Matthew 5:44
**Luke 23:34

On Peacemaking: A Litany for Lamenting Every Act of Violence

Diana Oestreich

The candles flickered and wax dripped on our mittens on the snowy street corner as we listened to the name of a boy who was killed. His mama described how his smile lit up a room and mentioned how proud she was that Mike was headed to college. "Say his name," the leader called out. "Michael Brown," I whispered in response as hot tears flooded my cheeks. Two little boys held onto each of my hands, tiny mittens wrapped in mine. Little voices raised up into the night saying the name, saying his name, to say his life mattered.

As a mother of a beautiful boy with dark eyes and ebony skin, I was scared. Five years earlier, I held my two-year-old son in my arms, introducing him to his new baby brother. It didn't matter that my family and I had been flying for the past twenty-four hours from Ethiopia to Minnesota; that moment was electric. Emotions hit me like a tidal wave that made my knees tremble under the weight of this newfound joy. Starry-eyed, I welcomed my new son into a family, childhood, and country, envisioning a peaceful life of lazy naps and cuddling on the couch. I didn't want to see the dark clouds of violence and racism gathering at the edges of our life.

Michael Brown's mother showed me a pain I couldn't bear, offered me a glimpse of a reality of which I was privileged to be ignorant. Knowing that I can't keep my children safe or alive is a terror that gnaws at me in the best times and suffocates my soul at the worst. I had never been to a political rally, protest, or city council meeting, much less a vigil, until that night. The most I'd ever practiced my citizenship was by voting, privately in a booth, not even brave enough to plant a yard sign for a particular candidate. But when the call to show up came, I knew, mama to mama, I had to go.

I was more scared to go to the vigil than I was when I was deployed to Iraq. I felt vulnerable, making myself so visible in my community. Standing up for Michael meant some would assume that I didn't love my country or I saw the police as the enemy. Marching down the main street, holding lanterns and signs, felt terrifying. I knew that in other towns people had thrown things at vigil attendees. When I called a police friend to see if it was safe to bring my kids to the vigil, he flatly said, "No." I wasn't safe to publicly lament a life lost. Freedom wasn't found in our streets.

We lit candles and stood on the street corner underneath a starry sky. We said his name so his mama, God, and every person walking by would know that he was a masterpiece. Because when we lose something priceless, something valued beyond measure, we hold it up and publicly bear witness to its value. We bear witness to the truth that when a life is taken, we are made all the poorer.

Acts of violence don't start with our fists or a gun; they start in our minds and hearts. As we lament every act of violence done in our neighborhoods, cities, and country, we tear down the kingdom of death and destruction. We root it out of ourselves and cast light on it, taking away its power to lie, kill, and destroy. Darkness cannot overcome the light. May this litany pour light where there is darkness, illuminating the way out of the culture of violence.

ONE: Come and hear our pain, O God.
Come near and hear our complaint.
Violence is singing a victory song, and our arms are hanging limp at our
    sides.
Our tears cannot stop.[2]
Violence has cut us. Bleeding, we stand together now.
Make us brave enough to stand in front of violence and call it a thief and liar.
ALL: In your mercy, make all things new again.

ONE: Make us lion-hearted, roaring at the acts of violence around us,
More dedicated to the common good than our own preservation.
May we learn to place those who are hurting first and ourselves second.
ALL: In your mercy, make us brave again.

ONE: Make us mercy, calling to those committing the violence.
Like lost lambs living in darkness, drinking bitterness, disconnected from
    their true selves,
May we call them back to the fold, shouting loudly that they are created for
    life not death;
Kinship not killing; love not hate.
ALL: In your love, make us family again.

ONE: Make us plowshares, sowing peace by renouncing every act of violence
    committed by our friends, our country, or our enemies.

May we refuse to be weapons against our brothers and sisters.
ALL: In your power, make us peaceful again.

ONE: Make us fearless, relentlessly waging peace instead of war.
Refusing to accept any act that cuts, kills, and breaks down people made in
your image—
No matter if they wear the uniform of police officer, pastor, politician, or
soldier.
ALL: As our Good Parent, make us fierce peacemakers again.

ONE: For those who have laid down their lives for others
And who have joined God in the unseen kingdom.
For those who have died to the kingdom of death
And who have risen to life with Christ in their breath.
All: We raise our hope because joy comes in the morning!

The Dangerous Journey: A Litany About Migration

Cory Driver

Not too far from where I live by the sea with my family, beloved people are waging a life-or-death struggle. They have crossed the borders of several countries on their northward journey. They face one last crossing before they make it to the land they have dreamed of for years. A little bit of water, some fences, and a few guards are all that stand between them and achieving their goal. Some make the journey because they seek a chance to support their families through fair remuneration for their hard work. Others flee ethnic- and gender-based violence. In every case, however, the migrants look across the waters through the fences and see the promised land: Europe.

I live in Morocco and frequently travel to the Spanish enclaves of Ceuta and Melilla for work. Crossing the borders is not fun with the crush of people trying to get through, but neither is it overly onerous for me. I flash my US passport, and the crowd parts to let me though. I unquestionably have the right to transit this space, and I—and everyone else—know it. The migrants coming from sub-Saharan countries undoubtedly have more to gain than I do by entering these tiny outposts of Europe in Africa, but they receive no welcome.

Indeed, when thousands of desperate souls make a mass attempt to cross the border wall, they encounter multiple fences, dogs, border guards from two countries, and trenches deeper than the tallest person. But the worst part is the razor wire. Coils and coils of millions of tiny razors waiting to cut the hands and feet that God formed to shreds. There is some talk of removing the razor wire, but it remains as of this writing. In the meantime, desperation, hope, fear, naiveté, love of family, and family pressure drive the migrants to seek a better life across the bloody border. No wall or fence can keep them out.

The few beloved children of God who make it across the border run to the Red Cross offices to have their claims of asylum heard before they can be unceremoniously tossed back from whence they came. Some who are unable to cross the fences remain stuck, clinging to the razor wire that shreds their hands. They would rather be stuck in the in-between than returned to the

Moroccan side and be beaten for the crossing attempt. That is exactly what will happen, however. Still, they will try again.

As bad as the land borders are, the waters are worse. Though the Strait of Gibraltar between Morocco and Spain is fewer than eight miles across at its narrowest, thousands of men, women, and children have drowned in desperate crossing attempts here and other narrow places across the Mediterranean. Giant gray naval vessels from several countries now fill the thin places, seeking to turn back people undertaking the dangerous endeavor and lessen the deaths at sea. Occasionally they, and hundreds of volunteers in private boats, are able to rescue people in danger of death when the overloaded, underpowered human-smuggling boats capsize. Other times, migrating humans are simply set adrift by smugglers who have already been paid and have little concern if the migrants' journeys are completed safely. All too often, the waters are not a pathway to a better life but a final resting place.

All over the world, children of God seek to cross walls meant to keep them out and deadly waters indifferent to their suffering. Yet we, as God's children, are bound to all our siblings who are seeking better lives. But how do we take responsibility for them? First, we feel concern for them. Then, we must move to action to save lives in dangerous situations; lessen the existence of poverty and suffering that motivates dangerous journeys; and comfort those afflicted at every stage of migration. Our belovedness and inclusion in the kingdom of heaven demands no less.

ONE: God, our Loving Parent and Creator of all, your children cry out to you.
ALL: Those who pass through the waters, those who struggle across the land—God, be with them!

ONE: God, you carried the Israelites through the heart of the sea.
ALL: Lord, you escorted them across dry land with your fiery presence. God has been with us!

ONE: Remember when you led your people through the wilderness of Sinai.
ALL: Recall when you preserved Elijah as he fled through the desert. God, be present to save!

ONE: As Boaz received Ruth and Naomi and provided sustenance for them.
ALL: As Boaz welcomed the foreigner and recognized her as kin. God, train us to love!

ONE: God, your Word reminds us continually: We were strangers in a foreign land.

ALL: Lord, help us to have radical empathy for those who are unwelcomed. God, teach us to welcome!

ONE: Lord, you sent your Son who was not of the world

ALL: To rescue a dying creation and to teach us how to live. Christ, Hosanna, save us!

ONE: Jesus: the way, truth and life, help us to walk in your ways.

ALL: You told us when we love the stranger we are, in fact, loving you. Lord, help us to love the stranger, our neighbor!

ONE: God, create in us a compulsion not to stand idly by.

ALL: Lord, stir us up to holy action lest the blood of our neighbor be shed. For the glory of your name and the love of our siblings in Christ. Amen!

Falling in Love with Bodies: A Spiritual Practice

Stephanie Vos

No one believes me when I say I like my body. To deeply enjoy embodied experiences is a radical act—one modeled by a God who chose incarnation. That we have a God who lived inside a woman's body, washed the feet of his disciples, sat down to meals with strangers, and asked that the sick and suffering be brought to him only affirms bodies as a source of divine inspiration and wisdom. Yet so often our bodies are shamed and blamed, dismissed and ignored. While this litany isn't in response to an acute crisis—there may not be a Sunday morning when the dire news of the week demands these words—we cannot overlook the larger need for lament of disembodiment.

I write this as a Lutheran pastor, chiropractor, somatic therapist, dancer, anatomy teacher, and energy healer. All of my most divine experiences have happened in and through my own body. I have never been so connected to others as when we are sharing moments that began with bodies—maybe theirs was in a hospital bed and I was the chaplain, maybe we were dancing in the late afternoon sunlight, maybe I was being splashed by Lake Superior as I was meditating on her rocky shores. Most importantly, I write this as a woman who deeply loves her body—and as a woman for whom that wasn't always true. My appreciation and affection for my own body has been a revelation and a journey, one that I hope is nowhere near finished.

My invitation to you, as you bring this litany to life, is that you embody it fully. Don't rush the inhale and exhale; make it a real breath. Also, if possible, have the words on a screen and invite participants to be in contact with one another—holding hands or elbows touching. You can also include other preliminary instructions like inviting community members to stand as they are able and to rock slowly forward and backward on their feet, side to side, finding the edges of where their weight can land and then consciously finding that centered place where the weight falls evenly in every direction at once.

Alternatively, if it feels like too much to ask community members to be in contact with one another, invite individuals to rub their hands together, use their palms to squeeze their arms, move their legs back and forth—anything to bring attention, awareness, and affection to the body. This could be led by multiple individuals scattered around the space or by one voice. The most important quality in the leader is their ability to set the tone and hold the space—the availability to truly be present in their own body in the moment. If the leader is going through the motions, the community will follow.

———————————

ONE: When we abandon our bodies to be absorbed in our screens,
ALL: We return by our breath. *(inhale, exhale)*

ONE: When our bodies are overwhelmed with fear and anxiety,
ALL: We take care with our breath. *(inhale, exhale)*

ONE: When our bodies fail and disappoint,
ALL: We stay close to our breath. *(inhale, exhale)*

ONE: When our bodies cause harm and suffering to others,
ALL: We come back to our center with our soft breath. *(inhale, exhale)*

ONE: When our bodies are harmed and violated,
ALL: We take refuge in the calm of the breath. *(inhale, exhale)*

ONE: When we judge others and are judged by the appearance of our bodies,
When we use bodies to justify "othering" our fellow beings,
ALL: We remember that we share the same breath. *(inhale, exhale)*

ONE: When we are consumed by thoughts of how we'd like to change our bodies,
ALL: We marvel at the steady perfection of the breath. *(inhale, exhale)*

ONE: When we inhabit bodies of trauma and histories of abuse,
ALL: We breathe for those who have endured before us. *(inhale, exhale)*

ONE: When bodies are dismissed and degraded as unspiritual,
ALL: We celebrate the incarnate God whose lungs were filled with breath.
   (inhale, exhale)

ONE: When bodies are demonized for their hungers and longings,
ALL: We celebrate our capacity to delight and share breath. *(inhale, exhale)*

ONE: When sex and intimacy are only ever painted with shame,
ALL: We rebel and enjoy the closeness of breath. *(inhale, exhale)*

ONE: When bodies feel like burdens,
ALL: We remember the incredible joys that come to us through bodies.

ONE: When bodies feel broken,
ALL: We remember that we always have something to bless the world with.

ONE: When bodies feel irrelevant,
ALL: We remember that our bodies are how we care for and relate to one another.

ONE: We value and celebrate bodies because God does—God who made bodies and said that they were good. Jesus inhabited a body; he knows what it's like to swim in the sea, to smell freshly baked bread, to hug someone he loves dearly. The Spirit is our breath moving in, through, and between us. It gives us life, moment to moment, freely and abundantly. Because of our faith, we proclaim the brilliance and beauty of bodies as spiritual teachers and ask God's help in remembering and reclaiming their wisdom and joy.
ALL: May our bodies be a blessing to us. May we use our bodies generously to bless the world.

ONE: Our breath brings us back to ourselves; our breath unites us with all beings. Through this embodied breath, this animating spirit, may we live and move and have our being.
ALL: *(inhale, exhale)* Amen.

Here Lies Love: A Litany for a Community Encircling the Grave of Someone Whose Life Was Tragically Lost

Osheta Moore

I'm sitting in a dark room listening to Yo Yo Ma and crying over the death of another Black teen I saw on the news—this one for playing his music too loudly. I'm remembering the teen boy in my community who was killed in a drive-by shooting and how the kids at the center where I worked grieved so deeply for him. I'm angered by migrant children dying of thirst and homeless people dying of exposure. I'm confused by the death of a mother whose daughters are still toddlers. I want to honor these lives by grieving their deaths well, but I'm overcome. I'm trying to remember Jesus—not only as the crucified one but also as the victor over sin and death.

In reality, grief is always breathtaking and core-shaking. Grief takes us completely out of our depth—no matter how much we try to prepare. Wearing sackcloth and ashes, lamenting and fasting, pausing and praying feel like the only appropriate responses. How do we carry our grief to Jesus when it's embedded in our soul?

As followers of Christ, we are not in uncharted territory. Jesus warns us, "In the world you face persecution. But take courage; I have conquered the world!" (John 16:33). He reminds us, "I am the resurrection and the life. Those who believes in me, even though they die, will live" (John 11:25). When grief comes, I want to acknowledge this truth while also not rushing to the solution of my pain too quickly. I don't want Jesus to be victor quite yet. I want to know that he sees and shares my grief. So I think about the death of his beloved friend Lazarus and how he himself wept. I think about how death moved the Savior to tears.

I wrote this litany to remind us that though we lay our loved ones to rest and we feel a myriad of emotions, not a single one of them is foreign and unseen by Jesus. So take heart, friends. Let's gather close to our people and proclaim the goodness of our God in spite of our loss.

ONE: Jesus, you can empathize with us as we grieve. You, Lord, have sat with the trauma of loss. You know the anger, sadness, and confusion that comes when death visits your loved ones. You know because you wept for the loss of your friend. Weep with us today, Lord. We trust in you to meet us in this space. Remind us that we are not alone.

ALL: Come, Lord Jesus, bring us comfort.

ONE: Lord, teach us the power of lament, and give us courage to weep with those who weep. Surround us and those who have been shaken by tragedy with love and community. Give us new resolve to love ourselves and others fully.

ALL: Come, Lord Jesus, bring us connection where this death has brought senselessness.

ONE: We do not want to be lost in this grief and overwhelmed by the depths of our despair. We want to hear you calling us to a place of rest. Help us, Jesus, to nestle into the safety of your wings.

ALL: Give us ears to hear you whisper "I am here" to our broken hearts.

ONE: Jesus, our minds swirl with memories of our loved one. We cannot forget their laughter and their vitality. We cannot imagine life without them. We are stunned by the vulnerability of the body, the brevity of our time together.

ALL: Come, Lord Jesus, bring us comfort. We trust you to work all things together for our good.

ONE: Jesus, our Prince of Peace, true source of wholeness, true bringer of shalom. Our world is violent, and violence delights in inflicting wounds of suffering and grief. In spite of this, you have called us to be peacemakers. With wounded hearts, you welcome us into your work of binding the wounds of this world.

ALL: Wounded Healer, we choose to partner with you. Help us to be the community we need. Show us how to bear one another's burdens.

ONE: Jesus, our humble King, you are victorious over sin and death. For the joy of true connection with those whom you love and for the joy of reconciliation, you endured the cross. You faced death head on, and you won. Love prevailed, bringing joy from despair.

ALL: Come, Lord Jesus, and bring us victory over death. It will not overcome us because you have reclaimed the grave for life.

ONE: Show us how to take up our crosses by surrendering our pain to you so that you can truly connect with us. By not ignoring the depth of our suffering so that your Spirit may guide us back to healing. By resisting hatred, revenge, and division through seeking reconciliation.

ALL: We commit ourselves to you.

ONE: Let us join you in conquering death and all its effects. May we, in the wake of this tragedy, remember the presence of our empathic Priest, the healing love of our Prince of Peace, and the unmatched victory of our humble King.

ALL: Amen.

All Saints' Day: A Litany on Behalf of the Great Cloud of Witnesses

Rose Marie Berger

Since 1992, the members of the Catholic worker community Jonah House in Baltimore, Maryland, have served as caretakers for a twenty-two-acre lot that encompasses a Catholic cemetery that had been abandoned since the 1980s. Bit by bit, the community has been reclaiming the graveyard from the underbrush and overgrowth.

On one All Saints' Day, I visited Jonah House to quietly pray the litany of the saints while surrounded by that "great cloud of witnesses"—both living and dead. It was a stunning November morning. Sunlight filtered through the red oaks. While walking the quarter-mile track around the graves and headstones, I was unceremoniously shoved from behind—hard. This was my introduction to Vinnie, the three-year-old donkey. Despite what one might assume about the donkey because of its name, Vinnie actually is female. And she's very strong. After completing a few more circuits of the prayer walk, singing a version of the following litany—all the while Vinnie prodding me and me jabbing back between "Amens"—we reached a rapprochement. I walked with a handful of grass in my left hand, and Vinnie sauntered easily beside me, nibbling as we went. I felt like St. Francis, having experienced a victorious achievement in sacred cross-species communion. Somehow, we prayed the litany of saints together.

This litany is not an exhaustive list; it's meant to be adapted. It contains some saints recognized by the church and many persons who have served the cause of the gospel or the spirit of liberation throughout the ages. Not all persons mentioned are Christian, though all are Christ-like. Many of the names listed here will not be familiar to every congregation, but I encourage you to spend some time learning about and giving thanks for the lives of those mentioned. I also invite each faith community to use the month of November to tell the stories of those who are part of its great cloud of witnesses, adding the names of those known locally who have inspired the community members to live a godly life in the service of others. If pressed for time, choose one or two readers' parts instead of all three. This litany can also easily be set to a chant or other simple musical refrain. Animal companions are not required, but the whole earth does long to sing in communion.

ONE: We call to mind the witnesses who have gone before us in faith.

FIRST READER: Our parents of earth and life, Adam and Eve,
Mothers Sarah and Hagar, and Father Abraham,
Isaac and Rebecca, Jacob, Leah, and Rachel,
Puah and Shiphrah,
Miriam, Moses, and Aaron,
Ruth, Naomi, and Boaz,
Daughters of Jephthah,
Daughters of Lot,
Dinah and Tamar,
Bathsheba, Uriah, and David,
Women of Midian,
Isaiah, Jeremiah, Hosea, and all Hebrew prophets,
Judith, Deborah, and Jael,
Pray for us.
ALL: Pray for us.

SECOND READER: The forerunner, John the Baptist,
Holy Mary, Mother of God,
Joseph, Elizabeth, and Zechariah,
Mary Magdalene and Peter,
Andrew and James,
Mathew, Mark, and Luke,
John, the beloved disciple,
Paul and Barnabas,
Anna, Dorcas, and Lydia,
Priscilla and Phoebe,
John the Revelator,
Stephen, the first martyr,
Perpetua and Felicity,
Pray for us.
ALL: Pray for us.

THIRD READER: Amma Sarah, Amma Syncletica, Amma Theodora,
Abba Poemen, Abba Anthony, Abba Macarius,
Mary of Egypt and Elizabeth the Wonderworker,
Matrona of Perge and Theodora of Thessalonica,
Basil, Athanasius, Gregory, and John,
Gregory, Ambrose, Augustine, and Jerome,
Teresa of Ávila, Catherine of Siena, and Thérèse of Lisieux,
Isidore and Maria,
Benedict and Scholastica,
Cosmas and Damian,
Dominic and Diego, Clare and Francis,
John Calvin and John Knox,
Martin Luther and Menno Simons,
John and Charles Wesley and Sarah Gwynne,
All you holy men and women, saints of God,
Pray for us.
ALL: Pray for us.
Grant us your wisdom.
Grant us your patience.
Grant us your courage.
Hear our prayer.

FOURTH READER: Our Lady of Guadalupe and Juan Diego,
Juana Inés de la Cruz and Bartolomé de las Casas,
Hannah More and William Wilberforce,
Frederick Douglass and Harriet Tubman,
Ottobah Cugoano, Olaudah Equiano, and Ignatius Sancho,
Sojourner Truth and Joseph Cinqué,
Angelina and Sarah Grimké,
Antoinette Brown and Olympia Brown,
Leo Tolstoy and Fyodor Dostoevsky,
Mohandas Gandhi and Abdul Ghaffar Khan,
Dorothy Day and Peter Maurin,
Takashi Nagai and the martyrs of Nagasaki and Hiroshima,
Agnes Le Thi Thanh and the martyrs of Vietnam,
Mother Jones and the martyrs of the coal mines,
Dietrich Bonhoeffer, Karl Barth, and Martin Niemöller,
Maria Skobtsova and Ilya Fondaminsky,
Etty Hillesum, Franz Jägerstätter, and Viktor Frankl,

Pray for us.
ALL: Pray for us.

FIFTH READER: Rosa Parks and Fannie Lou Hamer,
Abraham Joshua Heschel and Sylvia Straus Heschel,
Martin Luther King Jr. and Coretta Scott King,
Cesar Chavez, Helen Fabela, and the martyrs of the fields,
Mahalia Jackson, Duke Ellington, John Coltrane,
Oscar Romero and the martyrs of El Salvador,
Evelyn Underhill, Caryll Houselander, and Henri Nouwen,
William Stringfellow and Anthony Towne,
Howard Thurman and Sue Bailey Thurman,
Denise Levertov and Jane Kenyon,
Penny Lernoux, Jean Sindab, and Ginny Earnest,
Michael Brown, Trayvon Martin, Sandra Bland, Miriam Carey, and all
    #BlackLivesMatter martyrs,
Rosemarie Freeney Harding and Vincent Gordon Harding,
Dale Aukerman, Philip and Daniel Berrigan, and Ladon Sheats,
Tom Fox and the martyrs of Iraq,
Verna Dozier and Jeanie Wylie-Kellermann,
Maya Angelou, Amos Oz, and Aretha Franklin,
Juan Romero, Gene Sharp, and Marielle Franco,
Ursula Le Guin, Dorothy Cotton, and Miguel d'Escoto,
Pray for us.
ALL: Pray for us.

ONE: (*Invite the congregation to call aloud the names of the dead they want to remember.*)
All you holy men and women, all you kindred saints of God, pray for us.
ALL: Pray for us.
Grant us your wisdom.
Grant us your patience.
Grant us your courage.
Hear our prayer.
Amen.

Ears to Hear: A Litany for Listening One to the Other

Dee Dee Risher

I am a person of strong conviction and intense moral righteousness. I have a lot of ideas about how I think a "true Christian" should live in this world, and none of them is fainthearted. I don't think Christians should make much money, so they can ally with the marginalized. I believe we must live very simply to care for the earth—leave fossil fuels behind, grow our food, try not to produce trash. I don't think we should perpetuate war, and I feel racism and the love of money are major demons in this world. By now you get what I mean. Maybe you don't want to meet me at a party.

God's little joke is that many of the beautiful Christians I love deeply don't share any of these convictions. They may never talk about economic disparity or race, but they do care about cultural attitudes toward sexuality and reproduction, whether people are giving the Bible enough authority, or about people who are not Christian. They have a rosier picture of the legacy of my country, the United States, than I do. Never have we united around a political platform.

Then there are the people I struggle to love because they have done harmful or brutal things. And there are the people with whom I go 'round and 'round, never sure how they can think the way they do! (They return the favor.)

This litany is a prayer for divided times. It begins in silence and listening. It reminds us of all we do not know and what we must learn from one another.

(Prepare the group to begin in silence.)
ONE: Listen.
Hear your own breathing, the rustle of a neighbor's movement.
Listen to what is going on in this particular place at this moment.
Let every sound around you touch your ears.
(Pause)

Empty yourself.
The ancient teacher in the desert asked the disciple who was certain of herself,
"Do you want a drink?"
Then poured into a full glass of water more water,
Until it spilled everywhere and the disciple protested.
"Like the glass, you are full of your own opinions, ideas, truths.
You cannot learn to make peace until you empty your glass."
Empty yourself.
(Pause)
Job had many comforters, but when Yahweh came,
They were shadowed by mystery.
ALL: "Where were you when I laid the foundation of the earth?"*

ONE: O moving Spirit, displace us from our convictions
ALL: Into prayer.

ONE: Move us from our certainty
ALL: Into all we do not know.

ONE: Change us from warriors of righteousness
ALL: To people who know brokenness in ourselves and others.

ONE: Crack open our certain hearts,
ALL: Until we can whisper in the hollow spaces, "We may not be right."

ONE: If we could read the secret history of our "enemies," we should find
    in each life
ALL: Sorrow and suffering enough to disarm all hostility.

ONE: Love your neighbor as yourself.
ALL: This is the difficult Word of God.

ONE: Pray for your enemies and those who persecute you.
ALL: This is the demanding Word of God.

ONE: Do justice. Love mercy. Walk in humility.
ALL: This is the lifelong work of the Word of God.

ONE: May we see within our enemies and persecutors
ALL: Something precious that we ourselves need.

ONE: We commit today
ALL: To listen for what is under hate.

To sense the pain under aggression.
To look for the wounds our certainty causes.
To find the truth our opponents holds for us.

ONE: Like a treasure. Like vision.
ALL: Like the gateway from the land of the dead to the land of the living.
   Amen.

*Job 38:4

Frustrated Activism: A Litany for Those Whose Bodies and Minds Limit Them

Tanya Marlow

When I was young and dreamed about my future, I hoped to be married, a mother, and a full-time Christian minister with my husband. Almost twenty years on, I almost have that dream life: My husband is an Anglican minister, and we have a witty and bouncy boy.

I did not dream that I would be disabled.

Eight years ago, childbirth broke my body. I already had an autoimmune illness (Myalgic Encephalomyelitis), but the effort of labor tipped me into a more severe form of ME. Though I have improved since then, my energy is so rationed that leaving the house is a luxury I can afford only once every ten days for two hours at a time in a wheelchair. Before I got sick, I drank of life in big gulps; now, I must measure out my life in teaspoons.

Chronic illness shrunk my world: a bedroom, reading fairy stories to my boy, a little writing. My prayers were angry and inarticulate. Surprisingly, illness also expanded my world. Physical pain plus social media awakened something powerful in me: No longer mildly concerned about having a fair society, I felt every injustice acutely. I began using my writing to campaign globally for change—not only for medical equality for ME patients but also for disabled people and anyone excluded or stigmatized. Ironically, when I most wanted to act, my body prevented me. Campaigning is draining enough without an energy deficit too. I had to get creative. Being betrayed by my body robbed me of much, but it gave me sensitive ears to social injustice and a louder voice to challenge it.

What helps? Scripture offers relatable stories. The book of Job reminds me that sickness is great suffering. Those who also battle their bodies know the cautious optimism of tiny, slow improvements followed by rapid decline and the feeling of starting again at the beginning. But Zechariah tells us not to despise the day of small things because rebuilding the Temple seemed an agonizingly slow and impossible task—yet God made it happen. So too with justice today. The book of Romans gives us permission to groan when others tell us to rejoice, to weep while others pontificate, to be weak when the world looks for strength.

I wrote this litany for all who are struggling with sickness, mental illnesses, weakness, pain, old age, or other things ravaging their body. Rather than a lament, it is a blessing in the style of the Beatitudes. It is my wish that many communities use this prayer to honor valuable Christians with unique insights and extraordinary gifts *because* of their broken bodies, not despite them, and that churches bless even their honest frustration because it reflects the very heart of God.

The litany is designed to be read with the following formatting indicating each speaker:

Leader

All those whose bodies frustrate their activism

The whole community

ONE: Blessed are those who groan and long for healing.

PART: *Blessed are we who know pain.*

ALL: Blessed are those who groan, for the Spirit of God groans with them.

PART: *Blessed are we who cry, "It's not fair!" and "How long, O Lord?"*

ALL: Blessed are those who groan, for the Spirit of God groans with them.

PART: *Blessed are we who weep for ourselves and wail prophetically for the pain of the world.*

ALL: Blessed are those who groan, for the Spirit of God groans with them.

ONE: Blessed are the frustrated, who are left behind and miss out.

PART: *Blessed are we who would march but cannot.*

ALL: Blessed are the frustrated, for they echo creation's yearning to be free.

PART: *Blessed are we who would proclaim persuasively but cannot.*

ALL: Blessed are the frustrated, for they echo creation's yearning to be free.

PART: *Blessed are we who would leave our house and rally but cannot.*

ALL: Blessed are the frustrated, for they echo creation's yearning to be free.

ONE: Blessed are those despised and dismissed for their bodies and minds.
PART: *Blessed are we who are too much—or too little.*
ALL: **Blessed are the despised and dismissed, for Christ was also too much and too little for the world.**

PART: *Blessed are we who are too blunt, too weird, too emotional, too broken.*
ALL: **Blessed are the despised and dismissed, for Christ was also too much and too little for the world.**

PART: *Blessed are we who are not strong enough, not beautiful enough, not powerful enough.*
ALL: **Blessed are the despised and dismissed, for Christ was also too much and too little for the world.**

ONE: Blessed are those who live with limitations.
PART: *Blessed are we ordinary saints, neither heroes nor haloed.*
ALL: **Blessed are those whose bodies and minds limit them, for Christ was limited by flesh and shook the world.**

PART: *Blessed are we who are neither divine nor demonic but dearly loved.*
ALL: **Blessed are those whose bodies limit them, for Christ was limited by flesh and shook the world.**

PART: *Blessed are the creative ways we embrace life and speak for others.*
ALL: **Blessed are those whose bodies limit them, for Christ was limited by flesh and shook the world.**

ONE: Blessed are the invisible and unheard.
PART: *Blessed are we who see the missed opportunities.*
ALL: **Blessed are the invisible and ignored, for they see the invisible God.**

PART: *Blessed are we who raise our voices with campaigners online.*
ALL: **Blessed are the invisible and ignored, for they see the invisible God.**

PART: *Blessed are we who amplify the voices of the silenced.*
ALL: **Blessed are the invisible and ignored, for they see the invisible God.**

ONE: Blessed is the day of small things.
PART: *Blessed are the blanket-knitters and letter-writers, the poets and petition-signers.*
ALL: **Blessed is the day of small things, for God is rebuilding a home in our world.**

PART: *Blessed are we who chip away and pray and pray.*

ALL: Blessed is the day of small things, for God is rebuilding a home in our world.

PART: *Blessed are the weary who campaign in small bursts.*

ALL: Blessed is the day of small things, for God is rebuilding a home in our world. Amen.

Hope: A Litany Claiming That Another World Is Possible and On Its Way

Zhailon Levingston

I create new worlds every day. Specifically, I work in theatre, telling stories for the stage. My job is to look into the void of an empty stage and create stories of humanity that can be reflected back to the audiences for whom I created. It's my responsibility to turn the elusive into the material. I want people to walk out of the theatre saying they have had a real encounter with joy, love, despair, tragedy, triumph, and hope.

Hope, quite possibly the most elusive of these things, challenges me to turn its seemingly faraway song into an experience into which people from all walks of life can enter. How do I wrestle hope down from its hiding place, put meat on its bones, and offer it as a viable option to a room full of strangers? That's the magic of storytelling and world-building. In the four walls of my theatre, I tell stories of the least of us, centering their experiences and showing how people under the boot of oppression can overcome, all while maintaining a sense of integrity, humanity, and joy.

Hope filters into the equation when someone sitting in the audience sees themselves represented on stage for the first time or when someone in the crowd who doesn't think they will identify with my characters gets rocked by the multitude of ways they connect to the narrative being told. Hope reminds both the actors and audience that they are not alone. We all are connected by universal human need and struggle. But with great hope can come great doubt. Does the work I'm doing really mean anything? Because my Twitter feed and my news notifications keep reminding me that history doesn't tell a linear story, I often wonder why we still haven't learned the lessons of our past. Is this a vicious cycle through which we must keep going?

For every moment I feel myself slipping into the deep waters of fear and hopelessness, of depression and anxiety, my community reminds me that I am not alone. And if I just refocus my light in the direction of the people, places, and things that aren't given the same platform as my fears, I will see people choosing life in spite of death, creating things anew, and making the hope I seek as real as the air I breathe. I concede to my friends' reminders and pray to reconnect with the folks who are finding hope by building new worlds right here, right now—preparing the way for a better tomorrow and calling down heaven today.

"You can create something from this," says Truth. "You can create worlds with people where you offer grace to your demons and dance with your brokenness with hope at the center of it all." And this is possible for everyone, as we are all creative beings. Therefore, if we have the will to organize ourselves around stories that bring people together in their complicated and beautiful splendor, through creativity and imagination, new worlds can exist not only in the theatre but also in our homes and workplaces.

What stories are you telling? Who are you inviting to experience them? Where is your theatre? We all can harness the power of the artist to world-build because that power is the very nature of what it means to be human and what it means to be made in the image of God. We are made in the likeness of an eternal creative force that breathes new life into forgotten spaces in order to make another world right here within this one.

ONE: We are made in the likeness of Eternal Creativity.
ALL: Another world is possible and on its way.

ONE: Its insistence moves us into being and imagines for us worlds beyond our hopelessness.
ALL: Another world is possible and on its way.

ONE: We are made to collaborate with those around us to build deeper connections and sustainability around new ways of doing life together.
ALL: Another world is possible and on its way.

ONE: We are making space in our world for doubt and uncertainty by calling out fear and isolationism.
ALL: Another world is possible and on its way.

ONE: This is the truth about us. It always has been and always will be.
ALL: A new world is both here and arriving. We wait for it, usher it, greet it as a hopeful people. Amen.

Gaining One's Soul: A Litany for Selling Possessions, Giving to the Poor, and Sharing Our Lives

Lindsy Wallace

On Sundays, my husband and I, along with our five kids and a handful of friends, open our home for what we call "Family Dinner." It's a laid-back, potluck-style, open invitation gathering of saints and *aints*. One of us sings in the church choir every week; a few of us sleep on park benches every night. One of us works three part-time jobs to put food on the table; one of us turns tricks. One of us has a master's degree; one of us is a pastor's-kid-turned-drug-dealer.

One Sunday not long ago, a friend and neighbor rode his bike to Wendy's for salt, sugar, and pepper packets, then knocked half a dozen mangoes from a tree, showing up at our house requesting a knife, a bowl, and some hot sauce. He was his usual sweaty self, having spent the day foraging coconuts and mangoes to sell on the side of the road. I walked his bike around to the side of our house where he stores his (clearly stolen) shopping cart, fruit-picking tools, ladder, and a small bag of personal items. He sat at our picnic table meticulously shaving peels from the sweet, juicy fruit as other neighbors arrived, potluck offerings in tow. After opening each individual packet of seasonings and stirring the ingredients together, this friend offered my kids each a slice, blowing their taste buds and their minds. I carried the bowl, his offering, to the kitchen and placed it on the already-overflowing counter.

During dinner, we chatted about our days, my neighbor's and mine. We didn't have to draw similarities; they were as clear as the sparkle in his eyes. We lamented our frustrations with those around us and our frustrations with ourselves. He gave me the latest update on his battle with Veterans Affairs to get the hip surgery he needs, and I nodded in agreement with my own story of chronic pain and frustration over the labyrinth that is our medical system. "But you know what?" he said with a mouth full of fried chicken. "God is a good God." After dinner, rain began to pour, so my husband gave our friend a ride back to the park where he has lived for the better part of the three years we've known him. And though he'll sleep there again tonight and tomorrow, when I see him next, he will tell me again that our God is good.

For my husband, kids, and me, Family Dinner is a foreshadow of our eternal vocation as bread-breakers and other-lovers. It is a reminder that we don't have to wait for one glorious day in the future to experience the kingdom of God. The banquet table set for every tribe, tongue, and nation can be found here and now. If heaven will be filled with surprising friendships (which it will be), I want my living room to be too.

In moving to our city to live among the poor, my family and I have given up much of what the world—and the church—told us was necessary to live the American dream. But we have gained heaven on earth. Many a Sunday night, I have looked around my house—past the dirty floors, spilled drinks, and overflowing sink—with tears of gratitude and awe. I have seen the kingdom come, carrying a five-gallon bucket of mangoes.

ONE: For not being commandment-keepers,
For keeping up with the Joneses,
For jonesing for more and more and more—
ALL: God, forgive us.

ONE: For climbing ladders built by slaves
On stolen land with blood on our hands—
ALL: God, forgive us.

ONE: For building our own busted up empires instead of your upside-down kingdom
And viewing ourselves as *haves* and "those people" as *have-nots*—
ALL: God, forgive us.

ONE: For othering and running after the American Dream with more passion and fervor than we've pursued thy kingdom come—
ALL: God, forgive us.

ONE: For collecting shiny things, for furthering the wealth gap,
And for being complacent with the suffering of our neighbors—
ALL: God, forgive us.

ONE: For being enslaved to our possessions, our power, our privilege—
ALL: God, forgive us.

ONE: For mistaking what was never ours to begin with
As blessings to be hoarded instead of burdens to be given away—
ALL: God, forgive us.

ONE: For giving handouts instead of hand-ups,
The backpacks, shoeboxes, bikes, and Thanksgiving turkeys,
For stripping our neighbors' dignity instead of affirming it—
ALL: God, forgive us.

ONE: For our gluttony, our greed, our disbelief in the Beloved Community—
ALL: God, forgive us.

ONE: For becoming flesh and moving into the neighborhood,
For showing us the holy way of downward mobility,
For bidding us to come and see—
ALL: Jesus, we thank you.

ONE: For centering the margins,
For turning water into wine,
For dining with the "other"—
ALL: Jesus, we thank you.

ONE: For disrupting our pursuit of the American Dream,
For smashing white-picket fences,
For debunking 401k's that would have us to believe we don't need you or one
    another,
ALL: Jesus, we thank you.

ONE: For expanding and overlapping our lives with those who are financially
    poor
But rich in laughter, community, hope, and love—
ALL: Jesus, we thank you.

ONE: For revealing yourself to us in the faces of our neighbors,
For introducing us to our heavenly family,
For building a house with many rooms—
ALL: Jesus, we thank you.

ONE: For descending, incarnating, hanging as a naked enemy of the state on
   a hill among thousands of others deemed wretched,
For resurrecting us all—
ALL: Jesus, we thank you.

ONE: For showing us what it truly means to spend ourselves, share ourselves,
   and gain our souls.
ALL: Jesus, we thank you. Amen.

God Who Knocks: A Litany for Making a Home with and for Refugees and Migrants

Tony Huynh

Keeping people we don't know at a distance is easier than getting to know them. We can rationalize that getting to know a stranger may put us at risk and in the way of harm. Those who are strangers can hold untold secrets, hidden dangers, a multitude of evil. There are a whole host of reasons why we refuse to become familiar with a stranger. But could it be that by keeping those we don't know at a distance we actually are forgetting a common bond that we share? By keeping strangers away, we dehumanize them, thereby dehumanizing ourselves. Instead of getting to know people, we obsess over validating our assumptions about the stranger through data, numbers, and statistics. We move away from a culture of persons to a culture of things. Then we build more walls to protect our things, buy more guns to defend our walls, and vote for people who promise to protect our guns. We forfeit our humanity and become enslaved to our possessions when all we care about is keeping our stuff away from others.

Within the United States of America, the immigration system is inefficient. Not only is it inefficient, but it is broken and inhumane. We see people being reduced to statistics and numbers. People are seen as quotas: How many people are let in, and how many people are left out? What is more disheartening is that the church seems to be divided over how it should respond to refugees and immigrants. For those who profess that their faith is built upon the good news of Jesus, there seems to be much disagreement regarding what that good news is and who it is for. For a group of people who claim that their faith is built upon Jesus, we seem to forget that he himself was an immigrant and refugee.

Jesus is the God who knocks because he came into the world as a stranger, inviting us into a relationship so that we would be strangers no more. He knocks on the doors, walls, and structures that we have erected to keep others out. Jesus knocks as one who stands in solidarity with those we have rejected. Jesus knocks as every visitor bearing the image of God who approaches our front doors and southern borders.

When we look for Jesus, do we look for him in those we consider strangers? God calls us to love our neighbor, meaning there are no strangers. As followers of Christ who have been called and sent, we have an obligation to love those whom we consider the other. Jesus stands with those whom we call strangers and invites us into relationship with them so that we can be in relationship with him. This is the beauty of the gospel: It is good news for all because all people who were once strangers have been called family.

As we consider refugees and migrants, do we look with eyes filled with compassion and mercy? Do we not allow fear or self-preservation to hinder our ability to extend hospitality and grace? Jesus repeatedly extends his hand toward those who keep others away and calls them to join him as he stands with and beside the other. Today, Jesus is with those we keep out. Whether it be in our homes, schools, places of work, or nation, Jesus is with the outsider. Therefore, Jesus is with the refugee and the migrant. May we join him and stand by his side as he stands by theirs.

ONE: God of the caravans,
ALL: We pray for our siblings' protection.
Provide for them as you once did for your children in the desert.

ONE: God of the sojourners,
ALL: We ask that you give them shelter.
Protect them as they are vulnerable.

ONE: God of the travelers,
ALL: We ask that you guide them on their journey.
Make clear their paths and direct their feet.

ONE: God of the exiled,
ALL: We ask that you cover them with your wings.
Let them know they are not alone.

ONE: God of the immigrants,
ALL: We ask that you bless them and give them your peace.
Grant them passage, opening doors and borders for their entry.

ONE: God of the asylum seekers,
**ALL: We ask for deliverance from danger and violence.
Grant them liberation from war and poverty.**

ONE: God of the refugees,
**ALL: We ask for your mercy.
Remind us that you were once a refugee.**

ONE: God of the weary travelers,
**ALL: We ask for forgiveness.
Remind us to open our homes and our hearts.**

ONE: God who is their God, God who is my God, God who is our God,
ALL: Teach us to welcome all your children.

ONE: God who has crossed the border between divinity and humanity,
ALL: Teach us to leave behind our comfort.

ONE: God who took on flesh,
ALL: Teach us to love as you have loved us.

ONE: God who became human,
ALL: Teach us to be willing and vulnerable like you.

ONE: God, have mercy on us all.
ALL: Amen.

Kind and Brave: A Litany for Parenting with Love and Courage Amid Chaos

Erin F. Wasinger

Emptying my kids' backpacks on a Friday afternoon creates a flurry of information overload. My first-grader's teacher has sent home the snack calendar for the month. My third-grader hands me a permission slip and a note about a classroom party. (I'll sign up to bring napkins.) The fifth-grader's got math homework I'll be hard-pressed to help her with. Money's needed for Chromebooks and library fines and sports teams. Parenting is chasing paper, stuffing signed slips into color-coded folders, and remembering to buy snacks two weeks from now.

Lord, have mercy. I'm drowning in minutiae.

Moreover, on this particular Friday, my middle-schooler told me she needs new shoes, and I'm not sure I've got the cash at the moment. Another kid is upset over an "I'm not your best friend anymore" conversation at recess. And a small voice asks, "What's [the F-word] mean?"

Lord, have mercy. I have no idea how to navigate these waters.

On that same day, right before I picked up my kids from school, I opened a bill and shuddered at the amount owed. I flipped through a new issue of a literary journal, frustrated with myself for having not contributed the piece I'd intended to send in months ago. Then I scanned the pages of the newspaper but soon was disgusted at the refugee detention camps, the teacher who molested girls, and the nasty way politicians play the "I'm not your best friend anymore" game over and over.

Lord, have mercy. Take these weights.

Then I wondered, *How can I possibly teach my kids how to be brave and kind? to speak to their classmates with grace? to practice reconciliation on the playground? to respond to crises a half dozen states away? to swim in a river of peace when the world is pelting us with so much pain?*

Lord, have mercy. Save us quickly.

The following litany is for these moments—when we find ourselves worn down, tired, and confused, sitting on the couch with our kids and needing the words to pray. With the confidence of toddlers and the passion of teens, we pray these words to a God who invites us to experience peace—even peace amid chaos. Light a candle (or use a cell phone flashlight) to center yourselves, but let the kids wiggle, swing their feet, chew their gum, fidget. May their constantly moving bodies remind us of the never-ending energy, the continual tide of a new kingdom crashing into our lives. This particular litany's format is organized as follows:

Parent/Adult Leader
Children at suitable reading level
Whole Community

ONE: God, please help us—parents, children, neighbors, teachers, family, and classmates—to learn how to be brave and good.
CHILDREN: *So our homes, neighborhoods, schools, and playgrounds*
Would be places where people experience your love and mercy
Instead of our pride and power over others.
ALL: We pray together now as softly or as loudly as we want to, knowing that you hear us no matter where or who we are.

ONE: When I add to the tension of an argument by yelling,
CHILDREN: *When my body wants to fight,*
ALL: Spirit, help our words and actions reflect your patience.

ONE: When stress accumulates in a clenched jaw or an apathetic heart,
CHILDREN: *When I feel like nothing I do is good enough,*
ALL: Spirit, renew our energy for being courageous peacemakers.

ONE: When I feel outmatched by the depths of need at home and in the world,
CHILDREN: *When the world is scary and confusing,*
ALL: Spirit, walk with us when we don't feel brave.

ONE: When I'm humbled by my privilege or overlooked because of privilege I lack,
CHILDREN: *When I know something's not fair, but I don't know how to fix it,*
ALL: Spirit, guide our choices so we courageously bend toward each other.

ONE: When things I've done or left undone hurt someone else,
CHILDREN: *When I don't know how to "make things right" with someone I've hurt,*
ALL: Spirit, teach us to be courageous when we need to ask for forgiveness.

ONE: When I don't want to forgive someone who hurt me or my child,
CHILDREN: *When people, even my parents, make choices that hurt me,*
ALL: Spirit, help me practice courageous forgiveness.

ONE: When I encounter meanness online, on the soccer sidelines, or in whispers,
CHILDREN: *When a classmate is bullied, left out, or made fun of,*
ALL: Spirit, give me the courage to speak words of love and kindness.

ONE: When I feel as if I have nothing left to give others,
CHILDREN: *When I just need someone to hold me and tell me it'll be OK,*
ALL: Spirit, still our bodies so we can courageously pause for rest.

ONE: When I feel prompted to offer a neighbor my time and my heart,
CHILDREN: *When I try to be a good friend to someone who is difficult,*
ALL: Spirit, mark us with God's kindness so we might be courageously vulnerable.

ONE: When I make choices that show love for all kids, not just my own,
CHILDREN: *When I offer to help someone or share my belongings,*
ALL: Spirit, may God's love speak louder than our small acts of generosity.

ONE: When your joy in our lives becomes contagious,
CHILDREN: *When we laugh so hard that we cry,*
ALL: Spirit, remind us that celebration is courageous love overflowing in our lives. Amen.

Gospel Reconstruction: A Lament for Slaveholder Religion and the Ongoing Racism That Infects Us

Jonathan Wilson-Hartgrove

In the name of "traditional family values," many white Christians in America have supported policies that separate families, suppress votes, and prevent poor people from receiving healthcare. Since the 1980s, the "culture wars" have focused much of Christian witness in public life on narrow cultural issues that have distracted from the biblical prophets' concern for immigrants, poor women and children, and creation.

Many millennials have been unwilling to accept the choice offered to them between progressive politics and orthodox faith. Many younger Christians see this false dichotomy not only as a challenge to their public witness but also as an impediment to their practice of faith itself. When slaveholders in the nineteenth century argued against abolition, they used the Bible to do it. But their lies not only hurt the people who were enslaved but also divided the church in America and distorted the spirituality of those who were taught that the Bible allowed some people to own other people.

I've worked with faith communities around the country to both name and unlearn the habits of slaveholder religion that still shape our souls, our faith communities, and our common life. This litany of repentance is an invitation to follow leaders of the faith-rooted freedom movement who have always known that we cannot separate love of God from love of neighbor.

ONE: Jesus, we confess that we have inherited a faith that was used to justify the theft of native lands and the enslavement of Black bodies. From this, our original sin, we ask for deliverance.

ALL: Forgive us for where we have failed to understand, Lord, and in your mercy, set us free.

ONE: Touch hearts that have been shriveled by generations of suppressed empathy and eyes that have lost the ability to see siblings who suffer from systemic injustice.

ALL: Forgive us for where we have failed to understand, Lord, and in your mercy, set us free.

ONE: Grant us courage to renounce the false teaching that we can somehow know you without being committed to justice for all people.

ALL: Forgive us for where we have failed to understand, Lord, and in your mercy, set us free.

ONE: In your mercy, help us mourn the divisions among the body of Christ and work for its healing in the places where we gather to worship you.

ALL: Forgive us for where we have failed to understand, Lord, and in your mercy, set us free.

ONE: Embolden us to resist the political forces that oppose the expansion of democracy by appealing to traditional values and idealizing a past when white men were in charge.

ALL: Forgive us for where we have failed to understand, Lord, and in your mercy, set us free.

ONE: As we name and unlearn the habits of slaveholder religion, give us grace to draw deeply from the witness of the movements that have always resisted injustice in the power of your Spirit.

ALL: Forgive us for where we have failed to understand, Lord, and in your mercy, set us free.

ONE: We give thanks that there is a river of witnesses that flows from Sojourner Truth and Frederick Douglass to Ida B. Wells and Howard Thurman; from Rosa Parks and Martin Luther King Jr. to the prophetic leaders who guide us today. Give us grace to follow them to freedom.

ALL: Forgive us for where we have failed to understand, Lord, and in your mercy, set us free. Amen.

We Call Your Name: A Prayer for Replenishing the Soul of the Activist

Gary Francis

This is a litany for the night. It is a prayer for those who choose to gather together after the heavy work is done or when it is paused. It is a litany for ministers, activists, nonprofit workers, and children of God in all walks of life who are laboring and resting in justice as it is in heaven.

This litany represents a communal voice choosing, again, Jesus as Lord of everything. It is a statement of loyalty to Christ above all temptations, distractions, and idols—and among all grief, weariness, and confusion—that the night offers when we are spent from the often hard work of doing God's will. It is a call into the communal confirmation that Jesus is indeed Lord—of even this.

———————

ONE: We sit in silence before we utter your name.
ALL: *(Silence)*

ONE: Lord, Lord.
ALL: We call your name: Lord, Lord.

ONE: We repeat your words today:
ALL: "Come to me, all you that are weary and are carrying heavy burdens, and I will give you rest. Take my yoke upon you and learn from me; for I am gentle and humble in heart, and you will find rest for your souls. For my yoke is easy, and my burden is light."*

ONE: We contemplate these words in silence.
ALL: *(Silence)*

ONE: Lord, Lord.
ALL: We call your name: Lord, Lord.

ONE: We say today:
ALL: You are Lord.

ONE: Who is Lord?
ALL: God is Lord of all. There is none like you. To you only do we reserve this name. We proclaim that you alone have complete authority over our lives. We submit to your supreme control. We submit to your will. We walk in your way. We acknowledge you as our source of life, breath, purpose, and love.

ONE: Lord, Lord.
ALL: We call your name: Lord, Lord.

ONE: We say today:
ALL: We confess and reaffirm our allegiance to you and you alone.

ONE: What do we confess and reaffirm?
ALL: We confess that we are prone to stray from our home. We confess that we are susceptible to roam alone. We confess that we are enticed to be idle and to be led astray by idols. We cry out that we are tired, hopeless, scattered, and burnt-out.

ONE: We profess that you are our source. You provide all that we need. We reaffirm our vow to take up our cross and follow you daily. You are the pearl of great price. Again, we place our fishing nets, careers, accomplishments, successes, and failures at your feet.
ALL: We call your name: Lord, Lord.

ONE: We say today:
ALL: We will gather together to breathe deeply, drink deeply, think deeply on your truth during the night. Then we will go where you send us tomorrow.

ONE: And tomorrow, where will you send us?
ALL: To where you can be found: in the margins of society, amid the unwanted. You are found in a people haunted, daunted with doubts and fears. You draw us near to those who lie on streets. People who are found on the outside of the boundaries of normalcy. Those with a proclivity to be labeled disabled or unable.

ONE: For those who are unable to live past paycheck-to-paycheck living, who embrace looks of shame and inherit blame and live under the oppression of the rat race of the same old, same old same—

For them you came. And so will we.

ALL: But only in your power, Lord. It sustains us, Lord. As it has sustained us all this time.

ONE: We say today:

ALL: You are Lord!

ONE: Who is Lord?

All: You alone are Lord! Amen.

*Matthew 11:28-30

Stewards of Our Home: A Litany for Our Interdependent Relationship with All of Creation

Kaitlin Curtice

I've never been a very good gardener. In all my efforts to have a beautiful, full garden, I often end up with half a crop at best. Some vegetables never see the surface. In other words, I'm still learning. But while gardening requires research and work, it's also a deeply spiritual practice. It requires a gentle spirit, conversations with dirt and seedlings, and a lot of prayer. When my two children sing to our seeds, the ones that are deep in the dirt waiting to be born, they are learning that the Earth listens. She listens and she speaks. She tells stories. She fosters life again and again for us, and we are stewards of that life, lives that belong to the goodness of God.

So when we garden or when we walk on the sidewalk outside our apartment building, we should wonder why there is so much concrete. We should wonder if it is hard for the birds to land when there are no more trees. We should wonder what life is like for all the creatures that we see and cannot see because we can't practice hospitality with one another if we can't practice it with the Earth. It is connected to working toward justice.

We don't own the land that we live on. Even if we've bought the perfect home with the perfect patch of grass, a few acres right outside the city limits, we don't own that land. It's impossible to own the land that sacredly lives and breathes beneath our feet or to own the sky that holds the clouds and sun and moon over us. We build our homes over land that was never meant to be owned, and we forget. We pull out our checkbooks and we pile up our debt because we are consumers. We are entitled. We miss out on the reality that the water and the ground—this Earth that is capable of such rich relationship—want to teach us.

To be a true steward of a truly hospitable home means we must remember that sacredness. It means we remember the indigenous peoples who originally lived on the land we currently inhabit. We must honor their lives because they honored the land. To be "environmentalists" means the church must join indigenous peoples in caring for this Earth. Because without her, we do not breathe. Without her, we know nothing of God.

When we go out to the garden and plant those seeds, we do eternal work. We join the Earth in sacredness. When we watch leaves fall from trees in autumn, we watch the sacred circle of life do its work. We join in something holy. When we have our friends over for a meal, we practice hospitality, which is exactly what Mother Earth has practiced with us for centuries, no matter how we've treated her. And receiving her hospitality requires that we remind ourselves that we are dust to dust. This isn't a sentiment we should practice only during Lent but all year long, throughout our lives. We should remember that we belong to the Earth because she gives pieces of herself to create us, to shape us, to teach us, to care for us. She is a constant giver, and so we are constantly being given good gifts that nurture life and love.

So we say these words together to do the work of constant remembering that we are simply partners to this good Earth that holds us. She is our best and most humble teacher.

ONE: We long to know the Earth in the intimate ways she's known us. We long to be the kind of people who listen more than we speak. May we always be listening.

ALL: Because we are dust to dust.

ONE: We repent of the ways we have chosen to fill our pockets with money instead of our souls with the goodness of the Earth. May we change our ways. May we honor her.

ALL: Because we are dust to dust.

ONE: We acknowledge the indigenous peoples who have always cared for the land. We acknowledge that we must learn from them, honor their stories, and pay attention to a deeper kind of relationship. May we dig deeper.

ALL: Because we are dust to dust.

ONE: We hope for a future in which we are hospitable because the Earth is hospitable. We long for a future in which our relationship is born out of constant connectedness, so that when we care for one another, we are caring for her. May hospitality be our future.

ALL: Because we are dust to dust and the Earth has always taken care of us. Because we are dust to dust, we will recognize our place in this world. Because we are dust to dust, we will choose, every day, to remember. Amen.

When Holy Days Are Hurting Days: Christmas Litany Amid Wars and Rumors of War & Easter Litany for Long Nights of the Soul

Rachel G. Hackenberg

"Tell the truth about pain," I invite retreat participants, and they share their stories of job loss and chronic pain, of traumatic memories and loved ones who've died by suicide, of faith struggling for hope and life wandering for its purpose.

"Tell the truth about pain," I invite a gathering of activists and ministers, and they speak of refugee camps and water shortages, of government corruption and human trafficking, of systemic racism and infant mortality.

"Tell the truth about pain," I tell myself, and the words pour out of my pen of paralyzing fear and quaking flesh, of violence and silence, of resentment and fatigue.

Jesus told the truth about pain—of denial and betrayal. Of mockery and derision. Of bleeding suns and roaring waves. Of birth pangs and wakeful nights. Of last breaths and torn curtains.

Telling the truth about pain includes those moments when our bodies cry out in protest against death and violence and the agony we cannot prevent from unfolding. Telling the truth about pain includes the heartbreak of silence and isolation, when the shame of fear and the fear of shame drive us into a corner, far away from the reminders of peace and joy, far away from the embrace of acceptance and wonder, far away and abandoned to chaos. Telling the truth about pain is a hard, honest, mind-body-spirit exploration of the landscapes in which God with us and God for us find their meaning: the ashes that might be replaced by a garland, the mourning that might know dancing again, the parched tongue that might find its voice for praise. To further paraphrase Isaiah 61:1-4: "The landscape of pain is like an ancient ruin, a desolated city, a devastation of generations, but look—on the landscape of pain, the devastated shall rebuild and repair. God with us makes us incarnate displays of God for us, charged with bringing good news to the oppressed, comfort to the brokenhearted, freedom to the encumbered, parole to the prisoners, and hearty lunch to those rebuilding (including ourselves)."

Tell the truth about pain—not because pain is so fabulous to talk about but because pain, when shared, leads us to community. And community leads us to the work of hope. So when the community gathers on some of its most hopeful holy days—Christmas and Easter—we do not neglect to tell the truth about pain together.

Christmas Litany Amid Wars and Rumors of War

ONE: Like a newborn baby crying, our souls cry out to you, O God.
FIRST GROUP: The world is laboring hard over war
SECOND GROUP: And not laboring enough over peace.

ONE: We feel strained by the violence of humanity and helpless before the industry of weapons.
FIRST GROUP: What protection is a manger?
SECOND GROUP: What effort toward peace is a lullaby?

ONE: We listen to the angels proclaim, "Do not be afraid," but we are full of fear.
FIRST GROUP: It is easy to dismiss the arrival of hope.
SECOND GROUP: It is hard to believe a song of wonder.

ONE: If the world has no room for peace, O Emmanuel, then let peace be born within us.
FIRST GROUP: No matter the birth pangs,
SECOND GROUP: Let us be your sign.

ALL: To the glory of God in the highest heaven and for the sake of earth, let peace be born among us. Amen.

Easter Litany for Long Nights of the Soul

VOICE ONE: Sometimes the sun's light fails, and the night grows too long.
VOICE TWO: By the time dawn breaks, our souls are too weary to welcome it.
ALL: Come, bring the spices and oils.

VOICE ONE: Sometimes the trauma is too vast and the memory too painful.

VOICE TWO: When we try to attend to it, there is only an empty and echoing tomb.

ALL: Come, bring the spices and oils.

VOICE ONE: Sometimes death feels too definite and violence too prevalent.

VOICE TWO: Burying our souls deep seems the best option to stop the bleeding.

ALL: Come, bring the spices and oils.

VOICE ONE: Sometimes grief is a vast shadow, and despair hides the moonlight.

VOICE TWO: The sudden glare of resurrection can be too overwhelming to bear.

ALL: Come, bring the spices and oils.

VOICE ONE: Sometimes pain becomes familiar and love a distant memory.

VOICE TWO: Tears and bandages are good news when all else is taken away.

ALL: Come, bring the spices and oils.

VOICE ONE: Come, bring the spices and oils,

VOICE TWO: And now lay down these preparations for death.

ALL: Feel the dawn on your face and your skin.

VOICE ONE: Take your time. Resurrection doesn't rush.

VOICE TWO: Christ is here, calling you by name.

ALL: Peace be with you. Peace be with you. Amen.

Once Again into Our Doors: Litanies for Creating Community, Celebrating Community, and Lamenting a Community's End

Lydia Wylie-Kellermann

A few years ago, the intentional community to which I belonged died. I had thought I was committing the rest of my life to this little corner of southwest Detroit with these beloved friends. I was staking my vocation upon a dozen egg-laying chickens, an urgent cry for immigration justice, and rooms filled with fellow travelers or neighbors in need. For me, the ending was filled with sadness, regrets, and unbirthed dreams. But the ending wasn't clear. In fact, we all still live on the same street. Our lives are lovingly wrapped up together, and we still throw a fantastic block party. The joy of being neighbors is filled with gifts and gratitude, but we stopped being an intentional community that shared decisions, work, and dreams.

When did it end? When did that shift happen? That murkiness was harder than anything. I realize now that what I craved was an ending ritual—a space to stand with my neighbors to celebrate all we had done, to speak of our love for one another, to honor our grief and disappointment, and to allow ourselves to be open to the possibility of something new.

Over the years, I have longed for community until my body ached. I've known the abundant love of community. I've hurt people and made mistakes. I've felt the rage at piles of dishes and undone chores. I've been challenged and changed. I've grown to understand what it means to be more human. And I've fallen asleep on pillows filled with tears as I've said goodbye to people I love and grieved for what could have been. Through every bit of it, the Spirit was alive, and I give thanks again and again.

These community litanies are in part written out of a desire to make space to sit in those sacred, hard times as we give room for God to linger. And they are written in part as prayers to offer company for all of us along the road as we experiment in our own places and times with the ancient, holy work of building the Beloved Community.

A Litany of Longing for Creation of Community

ONE: O God of creation,
Who paints the world with wonder,
We summon you to be near
As we walk with a soul full of dreams.
There is an ache alive in our beings
To intertwine our lives
In the life of community,
Where the love is tender,
The work cries for justice,
And the walk is humble.
ALL: Love is nurtured between us, and the Spirit dwells among us.

ONE: O God of the incarnate,
Who takes simple bread and makes it holy,
We feel you on this ground.
May we learn the history we stand upon,
The neighbors that surround us,
The needs of this neighborhood,
The soil and seed below our feet.
May we be formed by the roots of this place,
And may this community bring life
Whose branches spread with beauty.
ALL: Love is nurtured between us, and the Spirit dwells among us.

ONE: O God of breath,
Who conspires with us even now,
We bring our hearts to the journey.
We bring our hands to the work.
We bring our gratitude for the witnesses
Who guide us in this ancient work
Of building community.
God, dwell here
In the beautiful and painful
Gift of birthing.
Breathe with us and through us.
ALL: Love is nurtured between us, and the Spirit dwells among us.

ONE: O God of love,
Who knit us in the depths of the earth,
Guide our discerning hearts.
Cultivate our patience.
Set free our imaginations.
Ignite our courage.
Let it begin.
ALL: Love is nurtured between us, and the Spirit dwells among us.

A Litany of Celebration in the Ordinary Moments of Community

ONE: O God of gratitude,
Who delights in the goodness of the world,
We give thanks today
For the lives in this circle,
For the home that holds us,
For the work that challenges us,
For the history that calls to us,
And for the gift of this life.
ALL: Love deepens between us, and the Spirit dwells among us.

ONE: O God of communion,
Who counts the hairs on our heads,
Help us to have the strength to honestly name what we need:
The humility to listen when we are wrong,
The courage to face conflict,
The trust to share vulnerably,
And the ability to laugh with abundance.
ALL: Love deepens between us, and the Spirit dwells among us.

ONE: O God of gentleness,
Who catches the snowflakes as they fall,
Remind us to be gentle with ourselves
When the dishes pile,
When we make mistakes,
When the work is slow,
Or when what we hope for does not come to be.
ALL: Love deepens between us, and the Spirit dwells among us.

ONE: O God of justice,
Who hears the cries of your people,
We pray for those who are in pain this day.
(names can be spoken aloud)
For those suffering under systems of oppression,
For those sick, dying, or mourning,
For our neighbors,
And for one another.
ALL: Love deepens between us, and the Spirit dwells among us.

ONE: O God of silence,
Who speaks into the stillness of our hearts,
We pause to listen,
To rest in your arms
(Silence may be kept)
Walk among us today as . . .
ALL: Love deepens between us, and the Spirit dwells among us.

A Litany of Lamentation for a Community's End

ONE: O God, it is time.
Like leaves that fall upon autumn ground,
There is a dying time for all of creation.
Bless this dying time.
With hearts filled with love, grief, fear, regret,
And yearnings yet unknown,
We turn off the lights and say goodbye.
ALL: Love lingers between us, and the Spirit dwells among us.

ONE: We are mindful of the ways we have hurt one another,
In words, in what we have done, and in what we have left undone.
We ask for forgiveness now.
Even amid that pain,
We know that we have loved and been loved
In the ordinary and extraordinary moments of our lives.
We proclaim gratitude again and again
For all that we are and the gifts that were given.
ALL: Love lingers between us, and the Spirit dwells among us.

ONE: We give thanks for this space,
For all those who have walked through these doors
And found welcome.
For tears and laughter,
For dishes and bathroom floors,
For the work and the dreams,
For the history this place holds,
And for what it will become next.
ALL: Love lingers between us, and the Spirit dwells among us.

ONE: We set one another free
To love, to live, to be
Always held by this history,
This place, and these hands.
Know always
That indeed . . .
ALL: Love lingers between us, and the Spirit dwells among us.
Go forth into the world, fully alive with the joy of creation.
Be who you were called by the Spirit to be. Amen.

On Parables: A Litany for Telling Stories to Bridge Divides and Build Empathy

Michael T. McRay

Once, I witnessed storytelling transform a woman. I'll call her Kay. She and some others had gathered for a Narrative 4[3] story exchange on the theme of immigration. In this type of story exchange, paired participants tell each other a true personal story and then retell their partner's story, using first-person pronouns, as if their partner's story were really their own. I paired Kay—a Black immigrant—with a US-born white woman about her same age.

Kay's story was weighted with suffering, and her partner wept through the retelling. Kay wept too. After we'd heard all the stories presented, I transitioned into group debrief. When my eyes met Kay's, she looked as if she could float up from her chair and through the ceiling. When she spoke, she said, "I feel physically lighter after hearing my partner tell my story, as if the weight of that story isn't just mine anymore; there's someone else to help carry it. And as I watched her struggle with the pain of my story, all I wanted to do was hold and comfort her. And I've now realized that's what I've never been able to do for myself."

This certainly is not the only such story. I've sat with an English woman in Northern Ireland who befriended the IRA bomber who killed her father, once they embraced the risk of hearing each other's stories. I've shared tea with a Palestinian father and an Israeli father, whose daughters were murdered in that decades-old conflict and whose shared stories of bereavement united them. I've danced with resilient women in Rwanda who were given safe spaces to tell their stories so they could begin returning to their bodies after the devastating sexual violence of genocide. And I've experienced my own life change after walking inside a prison for the first time and listening to the stories of caged human beings.

Sometimes, long stretches of misunderstanding and misplaced animosity divide us. Sometimes, those divides are even within us. And sometimes, stories are the best tools for shortening the distance. If done well, storytelling can be a place of curiosity, deep listening, and humility. In such spaces, transformation is possible. When we're interested not only in *what* someone believes but also in *why*, in how the experiences of their life have led them to their beliefs, we may find that people seem less like monsters and more like people.

We're living in a time of both crisis and celebration of story. Many in our society are peddling false, destructive stories about others among us. As a culture, we've collectively suspended our ability to imagine that the people across the picket lines might have stories worth hearing. We forget that people are people, and people have stories, and stories have common experiences, and common experiences can give rise to empathy.

At the very same moment, true personal storytelling is booming. We aren't just paying attention to experiences of personal storytelling; we're running toward them. It's like we're drowning, and stories are the air that lets us breathe again. Experiences like those I mentioned give me hope. Not because I think we can bridge every divide through story but because I believe it's as good a place as any to start.

———

ONE: Jesus of Nazareth, you told stories to shorten distances. Your parables opened worlds. You knew that no one could be fully defined by a story, and no one could be fully understood without one. Open us to the stories of others, ground us in the stories of ourselves, and shelter us through one another because it may be our only hope. For the sake of the world,
ALL: Amen.

ONE: Let us pray.
ALL: In the beginning is a story, and the story is unfolding.

ONE: Jesus of narrative, teller of parables, bless our stories to unsettle our prejudices.
ALL: In the beginning is a story, and the story is upending.

ONE: Spirit who accompanies, inspire us with breath and boldness to speak our stories.
ALL: In the beginning is a story, and the story is unique.

ONE: God of unity, draw us together with curiosity and humility because our story is theirs and theirs is ours.
ALL: In the beginning is a story, and the story is universal.

ONE: We pray for a world relentless in the pursuit of justice, compassion, and kindness.

ALL: In the beginning is a story, and the story is unending.

ONE: Bless us with childlike imaginations so we can be wild in envisioning the possibilities of peace because nothing holy is tame.

ALL: In the beginning is a story, and the story is untamed.

ONE: We ask for wisdom to know there is more common ground than we expected.

ALL: In the beginning is a story, and the story is unexpected.

ONE: We ask for the wisdom to remember that no amount of common ground will save us if we believe that difference is dangerous.

ALL: In the beginning is a story, and the story is uniting.

ONE: May we challenge the poisonous narratives that uphold our violence and craft new stories of collaboration rather than competition.

ALL: In the beginning is a story, and the story is the foundation to everything.

ONE: Divinity within us all, pour over us the patience and perseverance to hold with respect the experiences of those with whom we disagree.

ALL: In the beginning is a story, and the story is yours.

ONE: God of love, may we love ourselves enough to own our own stories with confidence and courage.

ALL: In the beginning is a story, and the story is mine.

ONE: In a violent and divided world, bless our differences to bear fruit rather than arms, for our humanity is bound together and our lives inseparably intertwined.

ALL: In the end there's still a story, and the story is everyone's. Amen.

We Need You: A Litany for Embracing the Divinity of God in the LGBTQIA+ Community

Brandan Robertson

For LGBTQIA+ Christians, one of the most destructive messages we have often heard in the church is that we are somehow fundamentally flawed because of our queer sexuality or gender identity. This message communicates that the very aspects that make us human, the very aspects that others would say reflect the image of God in themselves, reflect something impure or disgusting in us. This toxic message breeds death and creates division in ourselves, our families, our churches, and our world.

This litany is written primarily for LGBTQIA+ people but can be used by everyone to repent of our patterns of demonizing difference and call us into a posture of wonder and awe at the divinity of God reflected in the broad diversity of humanity.

ONE: In the beginning, God created all that is seen and unseen;
Every leaf and grain of sand, every living thing, large and small;
Every human being, unique among the rest of the Creation,
Reflecting the glory and the image of our expansive Creator.
And God looked upon the earth and seeing the multiplicity of humanity,
God spoke the truth that has been spoken over humanity since the very
    beginning:
"This is very good."
O Creator God, you have spoken this truth over humanity since the beginning:
"We are very good."
Forgive us when we fear difference, when we minimize diversity, and when
    we forget
That your image is only reflected within us when we live into the uniqueness
    of our identity.

Let us remind one another:

ALL: We need you, for in our diversity we reflect the divinity of our Creator.

ONE: O Creator God, forgive us for the ways that we have perpetuated exclusion,

Pushing others away from their rightful place at the table of grace,

Believing that unless others conform to our image of what is right and good,

They are not worthy of our welcome and embrace.

Let us remind one another:

ALL: We need you, for in our diversity we reflect the divinity of our Creator.

ONE: O Creator God, forgive us for refusing to see you in the faces of our enemies,

For choosing to turn our faces away from those who we do not understand,

For believing that until we all are the same, we do not deserve one another's compassion.

In the midst of our waywardness, reveal to us the path of grace.

Let us remind one another:

ALL: We need you, for in our diversity we reflect the divinity of our Creator.

ONE: O Creator God, help us not to believe the lies that are so often spoken over us,

That we are flawed or broken because of who we are or who we love.

Your love has shaped and fashioned us just as we are, and your love casts away all fear and shame.

In the midst of fear and falsehood, let us remind one another:

ALL: We need you, for in our diversity we reflect the divinity of our Creator.

ONE: O Creator God, when we have been rejected and cast aside by those who bear your name,

Call to our mind the truth that absolutely nothing can separate us from your love.

Not churches nor pastors nor parents nor legislation.

Nothing will change your love for us, and no one can change our position before you.

Let us remind one another:

ALL: We need you, for in our diversity we reflect the divinity of our Creator.

ONE: O Creator God, when we find ourselves recoiling in fear or pushing away in ignorance,

Remind us to lean in, to reach out, and to seek your presence in the face of our *other*.

For in the most unlikely people and the most disregarded places, your Spirit works most powerfully.

Let us remember that no one is a stranger, and everyone can be a channel of your light.

Let us remind one another:

ALL: We need you, for in our diversity we reflect the divinity of our Creator.

ONE: O Creator God, you humbled yourself in the person of Jesus, taking on the flesh of one who was rejected and marginalized because of who he was in the world.

May the life and light of Jesus guide us as we live into our unique identities.

When we face discrimination or oppression, may we lean all the more firmly into the subversive love he embodied.

Let us remind one another:

ALL: We need you, for in our diversity we reflect the divinity of our Creator.

ONE: O Creator God, help us to see you in all of the ways you manifest in every moment of every day.

Help us to see you in our others and help us to see you in ourselves.

May we live our lives to proclaim with passion that every single one of us is pierced through with divinity and that every aspect of our queerness is a reflection of your glory in the world.

Let us remind one another:

ALL: We need you, for in our diversity we reflect the divinity of our Creator.

ONE: At the end of time, God has promised to bring us all together,

Standing in our diversity on equal ground around God's banquet table,

Where every nation, tribe, tongue, sexuality, and gender identity will proclaim

In our vast array of language and expression the glory of the one who has created us.

There will be no more tears, nor will any division remain.

We all will be one,

Standing in the radiant light of God's ever shining sun,

And we will at last know for certain that we are all and have always been *very good*.

ALL: Amen.

Rhythm and Balance: A Litany for Anchoring and Energizing Justice Work with Sabbath, Contemplation, and Community

Onleilove Chika Alston

During a life-changing trip to Nigeria and Ghana in November 2016, I visited three African tribes known for observing sabbath long before Christian missionaries came to Africa: the Igbo, Sefwi, and Ashanti. All three of these groups lost people to the transatlantic slave trade. All three of these groups honored Saturday as a day of rest with such seriousness that anyone caught working on Saturday could be banished from the village. I was invited to visit these communities to teach their women scripture-based empowerment and to learn more about their culture for a book I was working on. In 2012, I began to observe sabbath, and as an African American woman and faith-based community organizer, I can honestly say sabbath saved my life.

After five years of professional faith-based community organizing in New York City, Baltimore, and Washington, DC, I had hit a wall. Stress-based allergies began to exhaust my immune system, and I was unsettled by the success-driven culture that equated busyness with ministry. I was doing meaningful work with wonderful people, but I knew something had to change. During this time, I began to learn about tribes in Africa deemed "lost tribes of Israel" due to their history, migration routes, and traditions. Prior to colonialism, these groups held Saturday as a holy day when no work could take place.

As I researched tribes—such as the Igbo, Ashanti, Ga-Adangme, Sefwi, Lemba, and more—I learned that in Ghana, the Ashanti called their God the "Saturday God" and the god of the white colonialist the "Sunday God." As I continued to research my own family's history, I found that we were taken from Nigeria to toil on the Alston plantations of North and South Carolina. The Alstons are one of the largest slave-holding families in American history. Part of the trauma of slavery is teaching each generation to work and toil twice as hard as white people to get half the benefits. This was the lesson my family and millions of other Africans (many who came from sabbath-keeping tribes) were given: work nonstop because your value is only in what you can produce.

In 2012, I prayed, studied, and fasted and came to the conviction that I should keep sabbath. Scripture and my culture confirmed it. Ironically, when I began to keep sabbath, I became more productive and powerful as a faith-based community organizer. My allergies subsided, and my work moved from being faith-based to faith-rooted—springing from the grace I experienced resting in the presence of Abba. As a daughter of slaves, sabbath is a revolutionary act. Many Christians sadly think sabbath is bondage to the "law." But this theological belief came from white men who never had to toil under the burden of slavery. Sabbath was created because our Creator did not give us an identity rooted in what we produce but an identity rooted in who we were created to be: bearers of Yahweh's image.

Let's reflect on the sabbath, putting ourselves into the sandals of a newly freed Hebrew slave who did not have any control over their work schedule in Egypt. For a newly freed slave, a day of no work would sound like freedom—not bondage. Now, let's reflect again on the sabbath, putting ourselves into the sandals of a newly captured Sefwi slave from Ghana whose people held Saturday as a sacred day of rest. For this newly enslaved person, not keeping sabbath on Saturday (though some slaves got Sunday off, tribes from Ghana held Saturday rest in particular as sacred) would sound like bondage—not the freedom of grace.

> The LORD said to Moses: You yourself are to speak to the Israelites: "You shall keep my sabbaths, for this is a sign between me and you throughout your generations, given in order that you may know that I, the LORD, sanctify you. You shall keep the sabbath, because it is holy for you; everyone who profanes it shall be put to death; whoever does any work on it shall be cut off from among the people. Six days shall work be done, but the seventh day is a sabbath of solemn rest, holy to the LORD; whoever does any work on the sabbath day shall be put to death. Therefore the Israelites shall keep the sabbath, observing the sabbath throughout their generations, as a perpetual covenant. It is a sign forever between me and the people of Israel that in six days the LORD made heaven and earth, and on the seventh day he rested, and was refreshed." (Exod. 31:12-17)

There is a connection between constant work and death—physical death, spiritual death, and even relational death as we do not have time for friends and family. Though the verses from Exodus sound harsh, does Yahweh put sabbath-breakers to death, or are their deaths the result of nonstop work?

Sabbath is a sign that the Creator sanctifies us—not our work or what we can produce. We are not saved, valued, or significant because of what we do. Yes, justice work is commanded by scripture, but so is rest so that we can heal and connect with the Most High God and one another. Sabbath is a divine pause that allows us to be refreshed by the ruach (spirit) to impact our world not through striving and busyness but through the transforming power of justice, love, and compassion. Long before Christian missionaries came to Africa, my ancestors knew this.

For me sabbath is an act of resistance against white supremacy and capitalism. It has connected me in a deeper way to the Creator, my neighbor, and myself. Let us follow the path of true grace, finding rest for our souls.

Note: Before beginning the call and response, ask the eldest people in the room for permission to proceed. This is done in West Africa to honor the elders among us.

- *Ago* is pronounced "ah-GOOO" and means "Listen" or "Attention" in Twi, the major language of Ghana.
- *Ame* is pronounced "ah-MAY" and means "I am [we are] listening" in Twi.
- *Yesu* is Twi for "Jesus."
- *Ase* (or *ashe*), from the Yoruba *àse*, is a West African philosophical concept through which the Yoruba community of Nigeria conceive the power to make things happen and produce change.

―――――――――

ELDER: Ago!
ALL: Ame.

ELDER: Ago! We welcome Shabbat and call all who are weary to come to Yesu, the slain but risen King, and receive rest.
We know that sabbath rest was even something needed by you, our Creator, when we read: "On the seventh day God finished the work that he had done, and he rested on the seventh day from all the work that he had done. So God blessed the seventh day and hallowed it, because on it God rested from all the work that he had done in creation."*
If you, Creator of the heavens and earth, need sabbath, how much more your creation?
ALL: Ame! We hear, and we will rest by resisting the culture of exploitation.

ELDER: Ago! Calling all who are anxious, exhausted, and overwhelmed.
Come enter the beautiful rest of our Abba.
Enter the Creator's jubilee of rest.
Enter into God's love and shalom.
ALL: Ame! We will enter in and welcome shalom into our hearts, homes, and communities.

ELDER: Ago! Yahweh, help us to know that our value comes not from our activity but from our identity, which is rooted in you.
Help us not to overwork to fill a void in our identity but to root our identity in you.
ALL: Ame! Yahweh, we need your help. Renew our minds so that we value relationships more than we value profit.

ELDER: Ago! Yahweh, we need your *ruach* (spirit) to dwell in us to give us the wisdom to pause.
Help us to see the divinity in rest.
Help us to see the divinity in community.
Help us to see the divinity in our neighbors and ourselves.
ALL: Ame! With the help of Yahweh and God's Spirit, we will pause to take care of our bodies, hearts, and minds.

ELDER: Ago! Yahweh, forgive us for valuing work over worship, profits over people, and the temporary over the eternal.
Help us to divinely pause, trusting that you will hold our jobs, ministries, households, and communities while we rest.
ALL: Ame! Yahweh, forgive us and help us to value what and who you value.

ELDER: Ago! Yahweh, bless those who cannot take sabbath because they are enslaved, exploited, or emergency responders.
Be with all those from Ghana, from India, from America, and beyond who are entering your sabbath rest.
Help us to remember that sabbath is a privilege to which we all do not have access,
But that a day is coming when your kingdom will reign on earth and all will be able to enter your rest.
ALL: Ame! Yahweh, we pray your kingdom comes soon so that shalom and justice can reign on earth.

ELDER: Ago!
ALL: Ame!

ELDER: Ago! May Yahweh make our rest sweet and our shalom complete.
   Ashe!
ALL: Ashe!

*Genesis 2:2-3

Note: *After this litany, share a meal of bread and wine (or grape juice) as the breaking of bread and drinking of wine is done during sabbath by Jewish and Hebrew communities around the world. For Christians, the sharing of bread and wine on Shabbat is the foundation of Communion.*

When You've Lost Everything: A Litany for Dark Times

Jeannie Alexander

Sometimes when we've tried every prescribed route for transforming souls or minds or systems only to hit wall after wall, blank stares, and willfully closed ears to the pleas, hopes, screams, and sobs of families in desperation, we are then ready to turn away and allow our hearts to take control of our bodies, to give them over fully as instruments of disruption and resistance.

Empire and its handmaiden, capitalism, speak the language of "reform," and thus those of us aching are lured into a false sense of hope, just enough to keep us satisfied for a while. But there is always a tipping point. We live in the time of children in cages guilty of no crime except their parents' hope. We live in the time of children in cages, guilty of shooting each other down in the streets—victims of hopelessness, multi-generational poverty, and multi-generational mass incarceration. We live in the time of white nationalism peddling fear to the ends of internment camps. Not somewhere else, here.

Indeed, those constructing a landscape of walls and cages proclaim God's vengeance and God's justice most loudly of all. But were we not told the Spirit of God moved upon the waters, and the Holy Spirit caressed with tongues of fire upon the heads of the anointed? Something needs to be spoken here, something needs to be said, yet the words are lodged, stuck as a scroll in my throat.

If we pray, we must pray honestly or not at all. So we pray not to a god of walls but to the God of the brokenhearted. We pray to a Mother God on our knees with tears of blood, tears of a thousand screaming mothers. I pray to the God of raging, broken women, women who still rise. We have no words for a placating god of reform, the tame god of patriarchy and empire. Our prayers seek to conjure the God of transformation, the God of revolution, the God of the wild, dark mountains, the God of fire and flooding waters soon to be unleashed upon those who refused to heed the warning signs.

When we have lost everything, we are free to speak the truth. We are free to speak the prayers of the untamed God, prayers never written down or spoken aloud in a church. These are the prayers passed from generation to generation of women on the margins; prayers passed along the underground;

the last and strongest ragged whisper of a prayer spoken at the gallows. These are the prayers for today. Let us not whisper them but speak them loudly with our actions, loudly with resistance and love.

ONE: We call upon the untamed God of the wild, whose name is so old it has been forgotten.
ALL: Untame and liberate us.

ONE: We call upon the God of the desert, the dangerous God of Jericho, of Sodom and Gomorrah,
The God who demands mercy not sacrifice, the God who demands hospitality to the stranger.
ALL: Make us instruments of love to tear down walls,
To set righteous flames on systems of greed and death.

ONE: We call upon God in all her forbidden names,
And in all forms that terrify those who proclaim themselves master
And who rule through fear and violence.
ALL: May our love for life give us the courage to die.
May our freedom inspire others to follow God's narrow path.

ONE: We call upon the God of common ground, beyond all notions of wrongdoing and rightdoing,
Where we meet one another on equal ground, where there is always enough,
And where there are no masters.
ALL: May we have the courage to relinquish control,
To live without fear, and to love without shame.

ONE: We call upon the God whom 10,000 years of kingdoms tried to make us forget.
The God of the edges, the margins, the shadows, the God whose name can only be remembered through action,
The God whose love was too dangerous to forget.
ALL: Make us the seeds of wild gardens to cover the earth,
Vines to pull down systems of oppression.
May we become the fruit of knowledge and our blood the waters of life.
May we become, may we become, may we become. Amen.

Perfect Love Drives Out Fear: A Litany for Sifting Through the News and Social Media Headlines

Bruce Reyes-Chow

There is no fear in love, but perfect love casts out fear; for fear has to do with punishment, and whoever fears has not reached perfection in love. We love because he first loved us.

—1 John 4:18-19

My mother's second husband was an abusive monster.

He was also my primary father figure for a significant part of my preteen years.

He was the kind of man who would say things like, "Are you crying? Do you want me to give you something to cry about?" And I would say, "Yes." He was the kind of father who would ask, "Do you want me to pull over, and you can get out of the car?" Then he would pull over on the freeway, make my mother open the door, and demand, "Get out!" And I would get out and start walking. He was the kind of father who would use a leather belt to discipline his child: bare-skinned and humiliated, only causing more defiance from me.

His "love" was anything but. It was a relationship built on power, fear, and punishment. Thankfully, I more than survived this time. In fact, there was much for which to be grateful. I am grateful beyond words that my mother had the courage to end that marriage. I am grateful that I so distinctly know what kind of parent I must choose every day *not* to be. Most of all, I am profoundly grateful for what I learned about love—that a love driven by fear, punishment, or power over another is not love at all.

Fear masked with a face of love deceives us into believing a false story about God and God's love: about who we are, whose we are, who others are, who God is, and what God's love means. We must not believe this lie because when we do, we miss out on the opportunity to know God's true love: love that sees us as complex and created beings; love that guides and nurtures us as life unfolds; love that weeps and laughs with us through the rhythms of life;

love that God extends to us far beyond our human imaginations and abilities. This is perfect love, God's love.

In today's political climate the ease in which messages of fear can infiltrate our world is unlike at any other time in history. Fear-mongering is obviously not a new thing, but the sophisticated and insidious ways in which technology and social media are used to spread falsehoods of fear demand that we be even more diligent in discerning if the messages sent are helping us to grow into God's intentions and love or are pulling us away from God and who we are supposed to be in the world.

I do not blame technology itself as it is only a delivery mechanism, albeit a powerful one. But the ways in which we approach the information that is delivered must be deliberate, fluid, and disciplined in order not to be overcome by the nonstop, heavy-handed, and scattered ways in which content is dumped in our paths. Sometimes we must engage in Internet fact-checking. Sometimes we must lean on trusted relationships. And at other times, we simply must unplug before reentering conversations.

I do not believe that total and permanent disengagement is the answer. There is too much at stake in the world to abdicate the power that we all have in our spaces of influence. So for those times when the overwhelming presence of fear-mongering and a glaring absence of messages of God's love are drawing us in, I offer this prayer for our communities.

ONE: We are told that God wants us to live in fear, to protect what we have, to hate the other, to believe lies as truth.

When falsehoods begin to overwhelm our spirits and we want to lash out or hide away,

ALL: God, give us the courage to believe that your perfect love is not driven by fear.

ONE: We are told that God's love is measurable and finite, that there are borders and boundaries between those who are and are not loved by God.

When we begin to see your love as a limited commodity and ourselves as its arbiters,

ALL: God, give us the humility to trust that your perfect love is freely given to all.

ONE: We are told that to be tolerant and loving means that every story must be given equal weight, taken at face value, and embraced as truth.

When we ignore our intuition, amplify falsehoods, and honor deceit,

ALL: God, give us to the wisdom to know that your perfect love demands our faithful discernment.

ONE: We are told that there is nothing we can do, that we are powerless, that things have always been this way, and that energy is wasted trying to speak words of truth to a litany of lies.

When we choose to avoid conflict because it's easier, to waste our voice in spaces of influence, and to justify our privilege,

ALL: God, give us the fortitude to step into the fray and speak your perfect love into an imperfect space.

ONE: God is love.

God tells us that we are loved.

God shows us that love is not fearful.

ALL: God's love is perfect.

With this perfect love, we need not fear.

Because of this perfect love, we love more perfectly.

This we believe. Amen.

Where Others Have Not Understood: A Litany of Resilience Among the Abuse of Power and Privilege

Iyabo Onipede

My participation in a theology program taught behind prison bars was the gift that helped me understand and reframe the concept of power as it relates to privilege. On the campus of Lee Arrendale State Prison for Women in North Georgia, I saw power in all its various manifestations.

A prison guard, unconsciously feeling resentful that inmates were receiving college-level classes in the theology program and unable to manage his frustration and fear at his dead-end job, decides to restrict an inmate from attending the daylong, once-a-week class in order to feel power in his life as he labored at a $10.00-an-hour job. *Power over.*

An inmate dares to celebrate her self-expression, knowing the risk of punishment, by using colorful cutouts from glossy magazines and a layer of floor sealant as toenail polish. *Power within.*

The scholars in the theology program decide they want to share a holiday meal with their teachers, Master of Divinity students from area seminaries. The scholars make burritos out of ramen noodles, adding Cheetos as cheese, packaged tuna, hot sauce, and instant rice into the mix, creating something that resembles hamburger meat. A box of saltines appears. The teachers, who cannot share the food of the inmates, also place their food, brought from outside the prison, on the table. Everyone solemnly bows their head for a prayer. Inmate scholars, beside their teachers, break bread together and share the sacrament. The teachers, who thought they were here to share their wealth of knowledge, discover that there is more creativity, joy, and resilience behind prison bars than they had ever imagined. *Shared power.*

Economist Kenneth E. Boulding and other thinkers have identified an infinite form of power known as *power within.* *Power over* is the limited, finite expression of power, and it gets us into trouble because it is used to oppress and exploit others. Often, blinding systemic privilege couples with power.

This toxic mixture harms not only the "other" but also the power-holder. The holder of toxic privilege and power is unable to live in the fruitfulness of *shared power*. Power was designed to be shared. When we choose to share power, we can collaborate and create solutions that benefit everyone. To share power, we must experience the humanity of the other. It heals and creates new life.

––––––––––

ONE: When the invisible "other," obscured by the blinding mixture of power and privilege, asks

To be seen as whole and human,

To be heard as valuable and precious,

To be received into the full fold of community,

ALL: Lord, hear their prayers.

ONE: As those who find ourselves maintaining daily lives that are distanced from our "other,"

As the ones who live unaware of our advantages and how that affects our movement, presence, and priorities,

As we who were born into the unseeing nature of privilege, set up without our knowledge or permission, for us to benefit from,

ALL: Creator, have mercy upon us.

ONE: Where we have not understood and misappropriated the power that you granted us,

Where we abuse such power when we exert it over others, with physical, emotional, mental, spiritual, and systemic violence and force,

Where we wield such power to feed our egos and create our identities around the abuse of power,

We acknowledge the generational and bodily harm to each person involved in the dance of this abuse.

ALL: God, we ask for forgiveness.

ONE: As we enter into the awareness of what abuse of power does to the abuser,

As we acknowledge how we've abandoned those over whom we wielded our power,

As we become aware of the neglect and the stinging isolation that we have caused,

ALL: Eternal Repairer of the breach, make us all whole again.

ONE: As we turn inward and discover seeds of power where you planted them, Holy One,

As we yield to the Holy Spirit watering those seeds, and

As we discover the mysterious Omnipresent in others as within our own fragile frames,

ALL: Great Mystery, please open the way.

ONE: We recognize that though we may be afraid to trust one another and to move toward shared and mutual respect, we choose to dig deep and have faith.

We yield to the Mystery that is at work.

We each make the choice to share our newfound power within by reaching out to others,

By showing love,

By being empathic,

By listening,

By sharing wealth,

By disclosing opportunities,

By believing the best of one another.

ALL: Waymaker, teach us how to relate to one another the way you intended.

ONE: We embrace the creativity found in shared power.

We delight in the newness that diversity creates.

We receive as holy the truths of others.

We honor the ideas, products, and intellect of us all.

We humbly receive the lived experience of the other as a precious gift.

We enter into the grace of sharing power with one another.

ALL: Triune God, show us how to dance together seamlessly that we may be one.

ONE: We acknowledge that the opposite of love is not hate; it is neglect.

We acknowledge that we are incomplete without your healing.

We acknowledge that we have not understood, and we release false knowledge.

We accept the sacred gift of resilience that is present where there has been abuse and suffering.

ALL: Eternal Peacemaker, we bow in awe before you.

Stir in us compassion for one another.

Counsel us to see one another as wholly human.

Teach us to embrace the preciousness of all creation.

Create in us empathy as we hear one another's lived experiences.
Plant in us a sustaining wisdom that brings healing and reconciliation.
Seal in us that eternal hope that is rooted in you.
In the Sacred Holiness that created us, redeems us, and sustains us,
We humbly ask that you, Our Great Lover, hear our prayer. Amen.

Take and Make the Space You Need: A Litany for Loving Those Who Are Angry at the Church, Have Been Hurt by the Church, and/or Who Feel as if They Have Outgrown the Church

Kenji Kuramitsu

Like many others, I have experienced a significant amount of "church hurt" in my life. Trauma is painful and can leave its imprint on our minds, bodies, and spirits. Yet the particular wounds that come from spiritual abuse at the hands of those who claim to represent God often imbue hurting people with a special kind of ache, a peculiar rejection. This litany is for those who have found themselves pushed out of a community of faith or relegated to its edges. This is a prayer for those whose dark or queer bodies; whose liberating theology; whose clothing, questions, passions, or emotions were marked as suspect and a sign of spiritual danger by those who were appointed to care for them.

This litany is for those who have found themselves back in a church, for those who don't believe they will ever belong again, and for those who have chosen to work outside of institutional Christianity. I pray all of these folks are able to find a spirit of healing and a balm of peace even in the presence of many hurts. May we, especially if we bear such wounds, experience healing and peace. May we find a community that loves and honors and challenges us in the rich and lasting ways that we have always deserved.

ONE: In the beginning of all things, the Spirit of God hovered over the waters of creation.
Hovered but did not enter.
Hovered but did not plunge in.

ALL: We too hover.

We hover at the edges of your holy places, on the outside of your stained-glass windows. We linger near the God-drenched soils upon which we have been told we cannot tread.

ONE: In making a home among us in Jesus Christ, God drew all people to God's self.

Drew together the crushed and forgotten.

Drew in the oppressed and the oppressor.

ALL: We too draw.

We draw our hearts closer to you in worship and praise of your goodness. We draw our own harsh lines in the sand and push others outside of them.

ONE: God has placed poetry and prophecy in the flesh of the faithful.

Liturgy, for instance, means "the work of the people."

The work of our hands, the sweat of our brow.

ALL: We too sow.

We sow in places that are soft and hard, coaxing good things from fertile earth. We sow where we are welcome and where we are not.

ONE: God dwells with you.

ALL: God dwells also with you.

ONE: We pray, God, for healing and deliverance from unjust and hurtful ways of practicing faith.

ALL: With great zeal your people did defend your name and cause great suffering.

ONE: We honor those who burn in anger at the sins of your church.

We weep with those who have been spiritually abused instead of cared for.

We celebrate with those whom you have grown into new ways of faithfulness.

When those who seek your face are put to shame, that is not your will.

ALL: That is the will of humans.

ONE: Your people have suffered all manner of injury.

ALL: Your people have wounded others in big and small ways.

ONE: We know that wherever we gather,

ALL: You hear us.

ONE: You promised that your burden is easy and your yoke light.
ALL: Forgive us for those times we have added to the burdens of others.

ONE: Whether we stay or go, fill our lungs with your breath.
ALL: Watch over our coming in and our going out.

ONE: And let us never depart from your presence.
God, have mercy.
ALL: Christ, have mercy

ONE: God, have mercy.
ALL: Amen.

God of the Process: A Litany for When the World Feels Like It's Burning

Aundi Kolber

I am convinced that neither death, nor life, nor angels, nor rulers, nor things present, nor things to come, nor powers, nor height, nor depth, nor anything else in all creation, will be able to separate us from the love of God in Christ Jesus our Lord.

—Romans 8:38-39

As I type these words, multiple tragedies have struck our nation. Everywhere, people are grieving and angry—again. Hate, bigotry, racism, othering, and loss don't always make the news, until they do. On these evenings, in hushed tones after the kids are asleep, I ask my husband, "Did you hear about this? Did you read about that?" I cry and ask again and again, *God, would you meet us all in this mess?* And oh my, do we need Jesus now as much as ever.

As a coping mechanism, many of us briefly lose our sensitivity to the pain of the world because it becomes overwhelming. As a trauma therapist, this is no surprise to me—we are physiologically wired to handle only so much pain before we lose our footing. Yet I believe God is tender toward us in these times and longs to meet us in the tension between our desire to lament and our desire to remain present and hopeful with our children and communities. May we hold onto the knowledge that Jesus always makes a way with us and through us toward healing for all creation and that there is not one single thing in this entire universe that can separate us from his love. I pray this litany will serve as a guide to connect to God in times when we are cracked open to the pain of this world.

READER ONE: God who loves us in every season, our hearts ache as we consider our world. Amid sorrow and pain, we know you hold us and love us.

READER TWO: You hold us in confusion.

You hold us in grief.
You hold us in trauma.
You hold us in war.
You hold us in political unrest.
You hold us in disconnection.
Gracious Lord, you do not celebrate our pain but offer us deep love.

ALL: Compassionate God, you hold us.

READER ONE: Lord, we acknowledge that you are a God who does not rush us through our pain. You are a God who made us for process. Like a gardener planting a seed and waiting for new life to emerge, you tend our bodies, minds, and souls.

READER TWO: You make a way for our growth.
You make a way for our hope.
You make a way for our restoration.
You make a way for our mending.
You make a way for us to love.
You, our Good Shepherd, make paths where none have ever been.

ALL: Loving God, you sustain us.

READER ONE: Jesus, just as you wept with Mary and Martha outside of Lazarus's tomb, thank you for grieving with us as we ache. You knew you would resurrect Lazarus yet shared in Mary and Martha's grief. We know you share our grief as we witness a world that seems to be burning.
Just as you ache with those who mourn, equip us to mourn with our neighbors. Help us to offer comfort and care to every one of your children.

READER TWO: Empower us to love well.
Empower us to see others in their pain.
Empower us to move past our differences.
Empower us to believe in your goodness.
Empower us to be who you've called us to be for ourselves and others.

ALL: Compassionate God, you hold us.

READER ONE: Holy God, we pray that in the ways only you are able, you would equip us to be a healing presence in our world. Move us to love well, to hold space, to offer compassion, to bind up broken hearts, and to embody your goodness.

READER TWO: Again and again we cry out.

ALL: We need you. We need you. Amen.

Never Again: A Litany for Rebuking Mass Shootings

Britney Winn Lee

Fourteen months.

That's all I have left before my son leaves the pastel-painted halls of the children's center that is attached to my work and enters public school. For many reasons, I have looked forward to this for many reasons: I think he will enjoy it, our neighborhood school seems quirky and warm, and I have missed the life rhythm of semesters, to name a few. But for one reason, I dread this inevitable milestone. And that demon's name is *mass shootings*.

My baby barely had been earthside for a month when a gunman opened fire at a movie theater a few hours away from our home. Four years since, I have yet to sit through a feature film with my husband without fighting a panic attack. "Know your exits," he says, always, to try and calm my breathing. I cry angry tears as the funny credits roll, confused as to how this is still the culture in which we live. But this is our reality.

I chatted about my theater anxiety recently with a friend whose son is a bit older than mine. He's been in big-boy school for a year now. She said that she had shared with a coworker how she cringes when she thinks about her child coming home for the first time and sharing that his class has been running drills in case of gunshots. "He likely already has," her colleague said with conviction. "They frame it as a quiet game of hide-and-seek at that age." As she relayed this tragic truth to me, I grew nauseated. Hating the world that necessitates such measures, I raged for an alternative. But this is our reality.

Six months ago, when my family and I moved into our new-to-us home, we hired someone with a high-powered carpet cleaner to get rid of what the previous owner's cat left behind—enough dander to haunt our sinuses forever. A professional-looking, middle-aged man spent hours cleaning away the allergens. Before leaving, a bookshelf filled with theological resources caught his eye. "How do you feel about the state of our world?" he asked my husband, Luke, and me. After living in the Bible Belt for many years, I know a question like that can mean many things.

"We have hope," my husband Luke calmly replied, moving toward the door to usher him out. Not understanding Luke's subtle cue, the man continued. For an hour and a half he spoke about what scripture says about America's immorality, how he would rather his babies be dead than have to live through what is coming, and how God had told him that it would be good to begin stockpiling food and AR15s. For weeks after this conversation, I had nightmares about dangerous theology married to easy access to weapons of war (not to mention our culture's infamous mental health stigma). And I felt, to say the least, very, very scared as I ached for an alternative. But this is our reality.

And . . . I desperately need it not to be.

I desperately need our children not to be plagued by one more year of sickening possibilities and the fear that insulates them.

I desperately need our mamas and daddies not to have to normalize one more report of drills (at best) and casualties (at worst).

I desperately need not to see one more headline of names of those whose lives were sacrificed at the altar of senseless violence and too-little, too-late laws.

I desperately need for those claiming "pro-life" to include the lives of the students of Marjory Douglas Stoneman High School, the moviegoers of the Lafayette Grand Theatre, the image-bearers at Pulse nightclub, and the babies and teachers of Sandy Hook Elementary School.

I desperately need for not one more presidential term, one more year, one more month, one more sermon, one more day to go by without the country and the church—filled with good, smart, and compassionate people—getting more creative about gun control.

I desperately need for this litany to never be used by another community, another soul, ever again.

So I write it as a rebuke, a holy protest of stubborn hope for the world that I need to be ours. With it, I say to this mountain, "Go throw yourself into the sea." That it might.

Since it must.

It must.

———————

ONE: God, what can we say? We are heartbroken and afraid. We feel exposed and unheard. We battle against rulers, against authorities, against the powers and principalities that wish to turn our swords into automated assault rifles rather than gardening tools.

ALL: This is not your kingdom come. This is hell.

ONE: We wring out our souls at the thought of having to speak aloud another name of someone lost to gun violence. But we will not allow them to be forgotten—these names that God knew as they formed in the womb, these names of those whose hairs were counted.

ALL: *(Voice the names of those lost recently or in the past.)*

ONE: Come, Lord Jesus, we need you. Help us be parable-tellers, relationship-builders, truth-translators in a realm where polarized political arguments keep us from having eyes to see and ears to hear the trauma that our children face.

ALL: **Veil-tearer, rip wide the cloth that keeps us from moving forward.**

ONE: Hear our plea . . .
ALL: **Never again.**

ONE: Hear our weeping . . .
ALL: **Never again.**

ONE: Hear our anger . . .
ALL: **Never again! Never again! Never again!**

ONE: Lord, we rebuke the systems that we have built that allow for such atrocities. Systems constructed by toxic masculinity, white supremacy, xenophobia, homophobia, dangerous nationalism that convinces some that they have the right to self-preserve at all costs, and dangerous theology that convinces some that they have a right and an obligation to do your bidding as the Judge.

ALL: **We confess that we have added to this mountain. It did not form by itself or overnight.**

ONE: Forgive me.
ALL: **Forgive us.**

ONE: Free me.
ALL: **Free us.**

ONE: Now we tell it to move!
ALL: **Move! Throw yourself into the sea!**

ONE: In the name of the Christ who turned death around, who made his enemies his family,
ALL: **We say never again.**

ONE: Never again, God. We beg that you will lead your people, called by your name, to humble ourselves and pray. To seek your face regarding gun violence, to turn from our wicked ways. That you may hear from heaven and heal our land. That we may never again fear another mass shooting.

ALL: Never, ever again. Amen.

Planting Seeds: A Prayer for Our Gardens

Josina Guess

The places where we put down roots and gather real and metaphorical fruit are places of hope. Be it a patchwork oasis tended by neighbors in an urban food desert, a backyard bed disrupting the monotonous lines of a manicured suburban lawn, or a diverse array of flowers and vegetables replenishing rural landscapes laid bare by big business monoculture, a garden is a place of beauty, sustenance, and delight. In dewy leaves of kale and vine-ripened tomatoes, in the presence of happy pollinators and busy children, we get a little taste of the goodness of that very first garden and the promise of a restored earth yet to come.

As we work for social and spiritual transformation, gardening teaches us patience, perseverance, and faith. There are things that we have the power to change: the quality of the soil; what, when, and where to plant; and what to prune and pull. Though we do our best, there are forces that are beyond our control: killing frosts, damaging hail, and devouring pests. Although harvests can be joyful times of community, gardening—like activism—can also be tedious and lonely without immediate, tangible results. The lessons we learn from our gardens can help us to cultivate beauty and sustenance in our hearts, homes, neighborhoods, and faith communities. In the face of toxic, life-threatening forces like oppressive systems, violence, and addictions, we follow the command that God spoke to the prophet Jeremiah and all who were living as exiles in Babylon: "Build houses and live in them; plant gardens and eat what they produce" (Jer. 29:5). It is an act of faithful obedience and subversive resistance to choose to care for a small patch of this earth wherever God has planted us.

This prayer can be read by a family, a household, a church group, or a circle of friends who have decided to plant seeds and harvest. The litany is designed to be used outdoors at the place where the garden is or will be. It can be read at any season but was written for the season of Easter in the Northern Hemisphere, which is also a good time for planting.

Blessing the Soil

ONE: Lord of heaven and earth,
You started us in a garden,
Formed us from that good dirt.
Every day you breathe life into our dusty bones
And pour living water on our clay hearts.
**ALL: Let us start here, let us begin together now with you, with this
    ground beneath our feet.**
(If possible, kneel and invite each person to scoop up soil in their bare hands.)

ONE: Though it may be heavy laden
With traces of lead paint and microplastics,
Hardened with blood-red clay,
Sparkling with broken glass,
Tainted with arsenic from years of abuse,
We trust that you have the power to redeem every inch of this earth.
**ALL: We are starting here, with willing hands and hearts. Bring your
    healing to our soil. Let's get our hands dirty with the work that you
    have given us.**
(Drop the soil back on the ground. Have a watering can, pitcher, or water bottle full of water.)

READER ONE: We remember the tears of ancestors, sisters, and brothers
    pushed off of this land. (Pour water in the dirt.)
READER TWO: We honor the bones of ancestors, sisters, and brothers pushed
    to work this land. (Pour water in the dirt.)
READER THREE: We lament the tyranny of ancestors, sisters, and brothers
    pushed by greed to exploit this land. (Pour water in the dirt.)
**ALL: Lord, bring your healing to our soil; get our hands dirty with the
    work that you have for us. Bless the sweat, bless the tears, bless the
    bones. May you bring life and redemption to the ground beneath our
    feet.**

ONE: Lord of resurrection, in your mercy,
Send earthworms and nematodes,
Rhizomes and protozoa.
Let them find a home in this soil.
May it be crawling with life that our eyes may never see.
ALL: Lord, bring life to the ground beneath our feet.
Let the dirt beneath our nails remind us of your resurrection power.
    Amen.

Blessing the Compost

(If you have a compost heap, this part of the prayer can be done at that spot. One reader can hold a handful of dry leaves or another can hold a bucket of food scraps and then add it to the pile. If this prayer is done after a meal, use the scraps from preparation or uneaten remains of that shared meal.)

ONE: Give us courage to dig, to stir in the scraps,
To dig deeper and let your light touch all that is dead:
The rotten failures,
The sour relationships,
The spoiled hopes.
Take the rinds of unfulfilled promises,
Let oxygen move between the spaces,
Let holy warmth and cleansing waters bring transformation.
God, in your goodness, we trust that you can bring good from waste, that
    you make all things new.
ALL: Lord, bring your resurrection power to this soil.
Lord, in your mercy, turn our hearts into good soil
Where seeds can take root and grow.
Lord, bring life to the ground beneath our feet. Amen.

Blessing the Seeds

(If possible, ask each person to take a sunflower seed—or whatever seems appropriate to your location and season—and plant it either in prepared starter pots [empty egg cartons full of dirt work well] or in a designated spot in the garden. Encourage each person to say a hope or a brief prayer as they plant their seed. Allow silence during this time as well.)

ONE: Unless the seed falls into the earth, there will be no harvest.
ALL: Give us patience as we bury these seeds.
Give us roots that are deep in your love.
Give us hearts that bend toward your light.
May there be a harvest, Lord,
That reminds us we are not alone,
That feeds the hungry and sustains our souls. Amen.

Children of Abraham and Sarah: A Litany to Celebrate Those Whose Names Have Changed

Austen Hartke

One night, in the fall of 2013, I sat down for a long conversation with my girlfriend. This was part of a series of late-night talks we'd had since I told her I'd been thinking a lot about my gender. We'd been dating for a couple of years at that point, and she'd known since the beginning that I didn't feel comfortable with the female gender I'd been assigned at birth. I'd always been what my mom referred to as a "tomboy," but it was becoming clearer to me that presenting in a more masculine way but still being seen as feminine wasn't going to cut it.

I knew who I was. I knew that I was the child of two self-employed parents, the oldest of three siblings; that I was bossy, curious, a voracious reader, a dog-lover, a seminarian in training for biblical scholarship, a Bible study leader at my church, and someone who hated Brussels sprouts. I also knew that I was male. The fact that the rest of the world couldn't see this and that certain parts of my body didn't feel right was distressing.

As I laid this all out in our conversation, my girlfriend asked me a question: "Would you like me to try referring to you with a different name and pronouns, just to see how it feels?"

I remember feeling so grateful for her willingness to try something new with me, while at the same time feeling self-conscious about all the fuss. "Sure," I said, "let's try he, him, and his for pronouns. And how about Austen for a name?"

Austen. This was one of the names my parents would have given me had I been assigned male at birth. I asked my girlfriend to try this name out with me, and she graciously did her best for the month or so it took until the name stopped sounding like someone else's and became mine.

My new name felt like a recognition of who I really was. It wasn't that I disliked my birth name—only that it had been categorized as a woman's name, and that just didn't fit me. Like a pair of shoes received as a gift that look great but are unquestionably three sizes too small, it's hard to tell family members about returning a present they've so carefully picked out—especially a gift that's been kept for twenty-five years. Quite a few people in my life disliked and even hated my new name and what it meant about who I was. During the year I came out as transgender, there were times when all I wanted was for someone to celebrate my new name with me—to feel the joy I felt when people used it.

Miraculously, I found a group of people who wanted to do just that. My little Lutheran church, made up of artists and grandparents and recovering addicts and single moms, agreed to hold a renaming ceremony for me as part of a Sunday service. They gathered with me at the baptismal font as we remembered my baptism; they laid hands on my head and my shoulders, reminding me of God's blessing; they prayed over me and they baked me a cake with my new name written out in blue frosting. They celebrated with me when others couldn't or wouldn't, and I will be forever thankful for that gift.

This litany is something I'd like to give back to communities that are looking for a way to celebrate with the gender-diverse people in their midst. May it give us the words to affirm our siblings' truth and a connection to our spiritual ancestors who took a similar leap of faith.

ONE: In ancient days, our God met Abram and Sarai, two people who thought their lives were at an end.

ALL: They believed they were too old to become parents—to become something new.

ONE: And yet God worked in them to bring about life and gave them new names to match their new identities as parents of us all.

ALL: We give thanks to the God of Abraham and Sarah, who brings life out of death.

ONE: One night a man named Jacob lay down to sleep, only to find himself wrestling with a stranger. Jacob was a survivor, but he wasn't good at relationships.

ALL: He thought he could run away from community, from God, and from himself.

ONE: But on the night Jacob wrestled with the stranger, he made a different choice. He refused to let go until God gave him a new name.

ALL: We give thanks to the God of Israel, who struggles with us and blesses our changes.

ONE: A fisherman named Simon was standing on the shoreline the day he met Jesus.

ALL: He thought he would spend his life catching fish, like his father before him.

ONE: But Jesus saw something in Simon that no one else could. He saw all that Simon would become and loved him into being with a new name.

ALL: We give thanks to the God of Peter, who rejoices in all that we are becoming.

ONE: O God of the universe, who numbers the stars and counts every hair on our heads, you know us completely.

ALL: Whether given or chosen, our names are inscribed on your hands.

ONE: Help us, O God, to love each other well in word and deed.

ALL: Give us the courage to try words that may feel unfamiliar or uncomfortable and to try again when we get it wrong.

ONE: We gather together to remember our ancestors who took on new names and to love our gender-diverse siblings today who trust in this same promise.

ALL: Creator, Redeemer, and Sustainer, come celebrate with us as we experience our newness, our growth, and our becoming.

ONE: Loving God, we pray together, in all of your most holy names,

ALL: Amen.

No One Alone: A Prayer for the Lonely and Isolated

Dana Cassell

In a world that feels increasingly isolating, in a church that often lifts up the biological nuclear family, it is good and right for us to remember that scripture addresses community. Christ's commands are not meant to be achieved by individuals, white-knuckled and solitary, but to be enacted by communities, catching, holding, and lifting up one another, woven together.

In our insistence on rugged individualism, we often fail to notice our siblings in Christ struggling with isolation, cut off from the body, neglected and alone. This prayer is for widows, orphans, new immigrants, single people, the terminally ill, the recently released from prison, single parents—all who find themselves outside the circle of care that is Christ-centered community.

ONE: God, who exists three-in-one, with community built into your very existence, remind us that you created us to be together, in community, bound up in one another's lives. Grant us the eyes to see the ones we have neglected, the pain we have not noticed.

ALL: God, who exists as community, who calls us to welcome the stranger and befriend the broken, hear our prayer as we lift up those who find themselves alone.

ONE: O God, we pray:
For the widowed friend, alone in a life built for two;
For the child without parents, reaching out for an embrace that won't come;
For the single mother, desperate for another set of hands;
For the new immigrant, climbing steep learning curves;
For the recently diagnosed, reeling from the news;
For the brother in jail, cut off from friends, family, and community;
For the sister who has lost her child, cradling her arms around empty space;
For the elderly neighbor, eating alone;
For the rejected, the isolated, the ones cast aside and forgotten.
ALL: God, hear our prayer. No one alone.

ONE: O God, we remember—

Your words at creation: "It is not good that [humans] should be alone."*

Your word in the law: "You shall love your neighbor as yourself."**

Your word from the prophets: "Religion . . . is this: to care for orphans and widows."***

We remember Jesus, who called his followers to feed the hungry, give water to the thirsty, invite in the stranger, visit the imprisoned, care for the sick.

We remember Paul, who could barely speak of your people without naming them as a collective, a community, not one and the other but one another.

And your church, in the beginning, that held all things in common, adopted orphans, surrounded the widows, accompanied the dying, made room for the last, the least, the lost, the lonely.

ALL: God, hear our prayer. No one alone.

ONE: O God, we pray, make us your church.

Make of us companions, accompanists, people who slow down and show up, friends who make space, scoot over on the pew, bring another chair to the table. Move in us, compelling us to sit with one another at court dates and doctors' appointments, to fill freezers with casseroles, to create carpools and supper clubs and babysitting co-ops, to teach English and job skills and emotional intelligence.

ALL: God, hear our prayer.

ONE: In your church, O God, no one is alone.

ALL: No one is alone.

ONE: Not widows, not orphans, not immigrants.

Not single people, not sick people, not people who've been released from jail.

ALL: No one is alone.

ONE: Not strangers, not victims, not perpetrators.

Speak to us again, God of the Trinity, God of community.

Call us back to our senses, back to one another.

ALL: God, hear our prayer. Amen.

*Genesis 2:18
**Mark 12:31
***James 1:27

Shared Creator: A Litany for More Grace in Interreligious Contexts

Stephanie Vos

sometimes tell people I'm in an open relationship with Christianity. I love so much of what I find there, amid the struggles that are inevitable in every intimate relationship. But I can't help falling in love with the truth, beauty, and wisdom of other traditions and spiritual paths. What can I say—I have a polyamorous spirit. I find wisdom in a Zen koan and a Sufi poem, in a Buddhist teaching and a Wiccan blessing. These pieces of wisdom sit next to one another on my shelves (and altar), and they bring light into my life and love into my heart. More importantly, they inspire me to do better and be better to the world, to my neighbor, and to myself.

So often we get caught up in defending our teachers instead of their teachings. We fight for the source rather than the message. We fall for the lies of a society obsessed with power-over and binary systems. We fall prey to fears and toxic tribalism. We fall into the traps that others have set for us. But as people of faith—of any kind of faith—our hunger for meaning and community is shared, and our curiosities and blessings can show us how connected we truly are. And we know that conflict, when it isn't resolved with violence, is how we grow. Our unity is not at the cost of our differences but strengthened by them. We seek expansion, not erasure. We affirm our oneness with all beings and know that no two are the same.

My hope is that this litany gives room for everyone to have a seat at the table and sets the tone for each of us, all of us, to learn and contribute with sincerity and open hearts.

ONE: We are drawn together by a calling larger than ourselves, a love beyond
   our knowing and naming.
ALL: We call this power by many names,
Including (participants speak the words and names they use).

ONE: This love calls us to be close—to one another, to all beings, and to the earth.
ALL: This love calls us to celebrate and affirm the multiplicity of creation.

ONE: Let us not mistake unity for uniformity.
ALL: Let us not mistake distinction for division.

ONE: We rejoice in the mystery
ALL: And keep our hearts open to new delights.

ONE: We welcome conflict
ALL: As a catalyst for curiosity and growth.

ONE: We refuse wrath
ALL: And will not let ourselves be limited by anger or fear.

ONE: We believe that everyone has something to learn,
ALL: And everyone has something to contribute.

ONE: We believe that generosity, kindness, and compassion are a better way to live.
ALL: We believe that our witness to the world comes through our shared life.

ONE: We warm ourselves at the same fire, we are nourished by the same earth, and we are soothed by the same waters.
ALL: We fall in love with truth, beauty, and wisdom in whatever form it arrives.

ONE: We honor those who have come before us and blaze a trail for those who come behind.
ALL: We commit to being expansive and inclusive. We seek inspiration and insight.

ONE: For the good of all.
ALL: For the good of all. Amen.

As You Love Yourself: A Litany for Forgiving the Theology and Actions of Our Pasts

Nikki Roberts

I've always craved love. However, this is not to say that I have received love graciously—quite the contrary, in fact. When people chose to love me, they first had to clear an obstacle course of sorts, being prodded and tested and doubted at every turn. Only then, after showing up at the finish line, did they earn my approval. Understandably, this affected my ability to maintain friends and intimate partnerships, and I found myself often feeling isolated and alone. Many years into my adulthood, I realized my inability to accept love stemmed from my childhood.

Growing up a preacher's kid came with baggage and pressure. And somewhere in my youth I did not feel validated by those in religious authority. I allowed those insecurities to affect the way I viewed myself, loved myself, accepted love, and even the way I saw myself spiritually. It took years for me to learn how to love myself—my Queer Christianity, my complex past, my poor body image, my weathered dreams, my trauma triggers. But it was worth it.

I can now freely receive the love I've always desired to have because I have embraced that I am not my past; I am a reflection of the love that Christ represents within me and within the way I love God's people. Love is one of God's purest gifts to us. John 3:16 tells us that God "so loved" the world that we were given Jesus. And Jesus demonstrated his love to us by becoming human, showing us how to live, and dying on the cross. Yet sometimes it's so hard for us to fully love our family or friends—and especially our own selves. I pray that this litany encourages others to love themselves and forgive themselves. It's never too late.

ONE: Merciful God of second chances,
For the privilege of being a beneficiary and a benefactor of grace,

Moment by moment, intention by intention,
ALL: We give you our gratitude.

ONE: For holy self-love and acceptance,
For wellness, self-forgiveness, and authenticity,
For wisdom and strength to confront with Light the dark corners of our pasts,
For courage to name and reject the bad theology that causes division
Among those who love, worship, believe, or think differently than we do,
ALL: We give you our gratitude.

ONE: For hands and feet to serve the poor and marginalized,
For hearts to show the boundlessness of agape love,
For eyes to see the needs of our elderly, widowed, parentless, incarcerated, and brokenhearted,
For open minds to welcome a broader way of accepting the holiness of our collective scars,
ALL: We give you our gratitude.

ONE: With humility that serves as genuinely as you have served,
With zeal of spirit for the fulfillment of purpose,
With laughter and dancing that declares resistance to oppressive and counterproductive evil,
With music and meaningful conversations that highlight your infinite goodness,
ALL: We worship you collectively with our gifts.

ONE: With restorative justice initiatives that improve our quality of life,
With actions that honor you as a liberating, loving, forbearing, accepting, nurturing Spirit,
With words that bring life, light, and love into ourselves, our families, our communities, and our nations,
With arms that open to those who seek refuge within our borders and to our neighbors we so often overlook,
ALL: We worship you collectively with our gifts.

ONE: With use of our personal truths and stories as testimonials to your transformative power,
With empathetic ears to lean in and listen, instead of listening with an eagerness to respond,
With special time set aside to care for ourselves through rest, reflection, and recharging,

With families we were born into and with friends-turned-family and all
   other definitions of family,
**ALL: We worship you, Spirit God, with gratitude and collectively with
   our gifts.**
**Use us—in spite of us, because of us—with great love for us and others.
Amen.**

Mirror: A Litany for Re-Humanizing the "Other" by Acknowledging Our Own Capacities for Good and Evil (and Our Own Need for Mercy)

Shannon K. Evans

I wanted to save the world but wasn't sure I even liked it. I was a more will-ing Jonah, perhaps, but an equally affronted one. *Here am I, Lord. Send me,* I prayed, knowing what the answer I heard would be—certain I was called to do the dirty work of picking up the lost and resettling them on the path of righteousness. What a thing it was to be one of the good guys.

Then those early years of motherhood arrived, and I felt stabbed in the back by the illusion of the woman I always thought I was. Suddenly, I had become someone who succumbed to anger, withdrawal, resentment, and a surprising ache for violence. Day after day I stood horrified and humiliated by the stubborn presence of my own shadow. I raged against the truth for two years before my soul fell into an exhausted heap of surrender. The only freedom to be had was to watch my pride disintegrate and blow to every far corner of a world that did not, in fact, "need" me.

Such is often the narrative of the Western Christian life. We enjoy imag-ining ourselves as conquerors when actually we are wounded travelers, stum-bling along a twisted gravel route in the footsteps of Jesus the Christ. We sing songs about victory with the relief of being on the winning team and take pride in the fact that we commit only socially acceptable sins. The cost of such delineation is that for us to feel like winners, others must become the losers. The mass culture of our Christianity dehumanizes the very flesh and blood that God became.

In this upside-down kingdom where the mighty are dethroned and the lowly are exalted, where the hungry are filled with good things and the rich are sent away empty, all our logic is flipped in light of a mercy so reckless as to prioritize the broken. If our theology does not dignify those on the margins the way that Jesus did, we have bad theology. And the greatest kindness God can offer is to break us.

When the breaking comes, may we welcome our shadow as it tears at our competency and snarls at our comfort. May we receive it as the gift that it is: a tragic, painful, necessary shedding of hubris so that we may see ourselves rightly. As we make peace with being image-bearers who hold both light and dark, both good and evil, we become free to make peace with the image of God in the other as well.

ONE: In our own darkest night,
We have seen horrors within ourselves,
And our bodies sag under the weight of our pretense.
Our disposition has been pious, hanging good deeds out to dry for the world
    to see,
But in the quiet, only we know the evil within our own hearts.
ALL: Lord, have mercy.
Christ, have mercy.
Lord, have mercy.

ONE: We have sought power in our homes.
We have craved prestige within our churches.
We have avoided the needy in our cities.
We have oppressed the weak in our nation.
We are broken yet do not admit it.
We are sinners and, God, we confess it.
ALL: Lord, have mercy.
Christ, have mercy.
Lord, have mercy.

ONE: We have cheered glibly of bearing Divine image.
And, yes, yes, our goodness sings out: It is so!
But there is more to the story.
Dualism has ceased to feed our souls
When our failures, our sins, our disillusionments
Have been the kindest mirrors we have held.
ALL: Lord, have mercy.
Christ, have mercy.
Lord have mercy.

ONE: When we were children, we spoke as children,
But now childish ideas have been put to rest.
Heroes and villains do not inhabit separate bodies.
Rather they war within each of us all day long.
As we look with condemnation into the eyes of the other,
We find ourselves pierced by our own reflection.
ALL: Lord, have mercy.
Christ, have mercy.
Lord, have mercy.

ONE: We repent for constructing a narrative
Where someone else is evil so that we can be good.
We repent for imagining an enemy in the face of a brother
When we might have had a companion on the longest night's journey.
We repent of our evil and we pray,
Lord, make us worthy to walk beside our neighbor.
ALL: Lord, have mercy.
Christ, have mercy.
Lord, have mercy on us that we may have mercy on others. Amen.

God of Many Names: A Litany for Loving Well Though We Do Not Think Alike

Chris Broadwell

How very good and pleasant it is when kindred live together in unity!" the psalmist writes (Ps. 133:1). However, those in communities that deal with various tensions (racial, political, economic, ideological) know that often the desire for comfort eclipses the need for truth. Paul writes in the fourth chapter of Ephesians to promote unity; however, this is not a cheap unity. We are not let off the hook from seeking truth and justice. Rather it provides an ethical framework for doing so as humble and committed followers of Jesus. It would be appropriate to read Ephesians 4 prior to this prayer.

ONE: Let us pray:
What do we call you, O God, you who are above all and through all and in
    all? What do we call you, when we know you in so many different ways?
ALL: Eternal One, Healer, and Friend:
Give us the grace to call on you.

ONE: Remind us, O God, of your faithfulness in gathering your people. From
    dust you created us, out of captivity you delivered us, and through your
    prophets you directed us.
ALL: Creator, Deliverer, Liberator:
Strengthen us to acknowledge our need to be made new.

ONE: Enlighten us, O God, to the ways we neglect your presence in our
    neighbors daily. But even amid chaos, destruction, and despair, you used
    a rainbow as a sign of your enduring love.
ALL: Light-bringer, Rainbow-maker, and Sun-stiller:
Help us to see your brightness in those we have mistrusted and mistreated.

ONE: Draw us together, O God, when we separate and segregate the body of Christ. You are with us and won't leave us to wander on our own.

ALL: Emmanuel, Prince of Peace, Reconciler:
Call us to right living with one another.

ONE: You have shown us, O God, your way, your truth, and your life. Yet we diverge onto paths contrary to yours.

ALL: Anointed One, True Vine, Good Shepherd:
Lead us onto the path of righteousness.

ONE: You have commanded us, O God, to pick up our cross and follow you. Instead, we have gathered rocks.

ALL: Redeemer, Resurrection, and the Life:
Teach us to value mercy over judgment.

ONE: Restore us, O God, and heal our wounds. We have been unheard, misrepresented, and attacked.

ALL: Advocate, Comforter, Sustainer:
Enliven us to care for ourselves as we care for your world.

ONE: Inspire us, O God, to live with all humility and gentleness. To persevere with patience, bearing with one another in love.

ALL: Rushing Wind, Fire, Spirit:
Consume us as we fellowship, sing, and give thanks with one another.

ONE: We know you by many names, O God, yet you are One. While we make every effort, we are not united by our own doing but yours.

ALL: One Spirit, One Lord, One God of all:
Above all and through all and in all, make us one! Amen.

Not Abandoned: A Litany of Friendship and Investment in Overlooked Neighborhoods and Schools

Brendan Blowers De León

What do we find when we visit the places that have been largely abandoned or overlooked by our society? The decision to go to those places is not made lightly. In choosing to leave behind comfort and convenience to walk alongside the weary and brokenhearted, we do so out of solidarity. When we turn to God, we discover that there is no such thing as a god-forsaken place but instead deserts where even streams of bitter tears can be changed into life-giving springs that nourish and enrich the city of God.

We can begin by asking, "Teacher, where are you staying?" And his response is to us as it was to his followers long ago: "Come and see." (See John 1:38-39.) When our lack of imagination dismisses these places and when we ask, "Can anything good come from there?" Jesus' disciples invite us to take a closer look. (See John 1:46.)

So, let's follow Jesus to where he is staying. Let's go and see the darkened halls of the schools we have abandoned. Let's cross the boulevard that separates one tax district from another. Let's take a bus to where the asphalt buckles and the homes begin to crowd together, to where we find a cluster of children kicking a soccer ball around in the dusty street. Let's look for him there, working under a neighbor's car or caring for a relative's kids. Let us be blessed to see him at work and to answer his invitation to join.

Part I: Praise

ONE: Lord God, we praise you for making what is hidden, visible, what is secret, known.
Nothing is concealed from your sight—

Not our sins and not the worth of those overlooked.
ALL: Lord God, you have searched us, and you know us.

ONE: You see what we hide beyond the boundaries of our neighborhood,
The people and the places we dismiss and disregard,
Those we push outside city limits where polluted rivers meet.
ALL: "Teacher, where are you staying?" we ask.

ONE: "Come and see" is your reply.
**ALL: You went to the places from which it was said no good thing could
    come.
The places labeled God-forsaken and abandoned,
We can now call God-redeemed
Because you have rebuilt them anew in your great love.**

Part II: Confession

ONE: Lord, we grow weary and our heads grow heavy.
Our bones are crushed by the pressures of our culture.
Our skin like the dusty, ashen roads we trod.
Our bodies slumped and our gait limping.
Help us before it's too late!
**ALL: We are too weak to change the division in our hearts.
We alone cannot change the people we have learned to be and the systems
    that benefit us.
So we ask you to free us from the bondage of everything that has been
    pressed and molded into us.
We welcome you in to change our hearts.**

ONE: We confess today that we have not loved our neighbor as we should.
We have shown favoritism to the one with the most money or power in the
    room.
We have seated the ruler at the head of the table,
But we have ignored those with whom you hold company.
We ridicule and belittle the humble; we ignore and mock the meek.
**ALL: We confess we rush to the seats of honor at the head of the table and
    trip over everyone in our path.**

Our pride is the garment we wear,
But we are better off naked before you.
Clothe us in your righteousness and justice.

ONE: The repercussions of our corporate sins are most felt by the poor.
But we hide the consequences in the unkempt corners,
In the darkened halls of our abandoned classrooms,
On empty playgrounds no longer fit for children.
Lord, have mercy.
ALL: Christ, have mercy.

ONE: Come and fill our hearts with your love.
For you alone, O Lord, are powerful.
ALL: And you alone, O Lord, are loving.

Part III: Reconciliation and Response

ONE: Can anything good come from "that place?" we ask.
ALL: "Come and see," you reply.

ONE: Lead us with your Spirit,
Show us where you are at work in places we thought no good could come
    from.
ALL: You have called us to follow you into those abandoned places in
    our world and in ourselves. We will go and see. Astonish us with the
    reaches of your love.

ONE: Lead us into the abandoned places of our city.
Lead us into the abandoned places of our hearts.
Leave no stone unturned,
No thought unexamined,
No corner hidden from the light of your righting and holy love.
ALL: May your light beam into our lives like the dawning sun through the
    slits in the tin walls of a refugee camp.

ONE: May your condemnation of evil and your reckless love
Pound against the walls in the hallways of our schools and disturb our sleep-
    ing streets.

Enliven us at the cries that rouse you to action, and break our hearts for what grieves yours.

ALL: Lord, we thank you. For in your love you have commissioned us and included us in the message and ministry of reconciliation so that your name will not be shamed but proclaimed among the nations.

ONE: Open our eyes to the needs around us, we pray.

ALL: Open our hands to the needs at our table. Help us to love one to another with the same love you have given us.

Part IV: A Blessing and Petitions

ONE: You have invited us into your presence.
We want to come and see where you are at work.

ALL: Thank you for the invitation to be both witness to and vessel of such good news.

ONE: We pray a blessing on those who have been abandoned
By the church, by neighbors, and by institutions.

ALL: We pray a blessing on those who have been left out by family and friends, by lovers and neighbors.

ONE: May your face shine upon us;
May you illuminate the dark shadows of our city.

ALL: May you bring fullness to our broken bodies and calm the angry spirits in our midst.

ONE: Lord, we ask that you change places of weeping into streams that make glad the city of God.

ALL: May the rocks and darkness cry out; may we not silence the hurting. May we give ear to their cry; may we not ignore their tears. Amen.

Will the Darkness Win?: A Maundy Thursday Peace and Justice Litany

Britney Winn Lee

Before reading James Cone's book *The Cross and the Lynching Tree* during the most recent Lenten season, I had not realized that the more "progressive" my faith has gotten, the more willing I had become to overlook the Cross as far as it pertained to my understanding of God. Raised evangelical, surrounded by the teaching of penal substitutionary theology and the emphasis that Jesus' torturous death was the solution to an angry God's rage at a rotten people, I (truly subconsciously) began to reject all things crucifixion.

This made Easter services quite important (resurrection and all) to me but caused the Good Friday and Maundy Thursday gatherings that preceded them to become rather faded in meaning—almost mythical. A God of renewal of the earth and hope for the marginalized could be found outside of an empty tomb—and that was the main thing. But, then, entered Cone's writings. And they said to me as a reader and a follower of Jesus, *You cannot skip the Cross and understand what the gospel means to the oppressed. You cannot skip the meal, where the incarnate divine washed the caked mud from the feet of his friends and betrayers, and understand enemy-love. You cannot skip the commission. You cannot skip the mob. You cannot skip the solidarity of God with those who are killed by the abuse of power and understand the resurrection. If Sunday is about God for Us, then Friday is about God with Us and Thursday God in Us.* We miss a lot by missing Easter's lead-up, when all was uncertain and it seemed as though the darkness would win.

This is a litany written for a Maundy Thursday service centering around peace and justice. Participants are encouraged to break up the many readings with communal singing.

ONE: God, we gather as an Easter people with resurrection approaching.

ALL: We remember, O Savior, that you stepped into death, oppression, and hopelessness, thereby giving us hope, liberation, and full life both now and forever.

ONE: But first, we must not bypass the Cross: your murder by the state and religious authorities, forever connecting you to radical martyrs, to people who speak truth to power, and to victims of fear and hate-driven violence. We acknowledge, Jesus, that your cross is not unlike the lynching tree, the refugee camp caused by genocides and holy wars, the terror inflicted at the hands of white supremacy, the abuse or threat of abuse felt by women the world over.

ALL: We remember, Suffering Servant, that before you conquered hell, you experienced hell. We can trust you as our Light because you have been with us in the most extreme darkness.

ONE: But even before we get to the Cross, we cannot bypass the meal. On the night before Jesus was taken by a crowd who, wrapped up in mob mentality, declared good news to be the enemy, Jesus drew near to his friends. Before God—in God's human form—concluded his physical time here on this earth, the last thing he did was gather with his people to eat supper. And to wash their filthy feet. To sit around loaves and cups, water and rags. Eating, singing, grieving, and declaring there to be a new commandment.

ALL: We remember tonight, Son of God and Son of Mary, your last gathering with friends. We remember that before eternal life and before the grave that it conquered, there was a meal, intimacy with God, and a commission to love the world as you have loved the world.

ONE: So now we follow you into Jerusalem, on your way to the table.

READER 1: (Read Mark 11:1-10.)

Your entrance was less triumphal than a world-made-for-war had hoped. But that is because you came to make us more than conquerors; you chose to showcase a world where love wins and no one has to be destroyed. You rode a humble colt, waved onward by a parade of peasants' palms. You were the people's King, turning power on its head and debunking the systems that forget the poor, that damage whole groups of God's image-bearers. Thank you for coming in ways we least expect. Give us eyes to see how you enter our world today.

READER 2: (Read Mark 11:15-18.)

You have demonstrated for us a righteous anger by toppling the foundations on which rest the people who manipulate the language and the sanctuaries of our faith in order to profit. You call out those who put a price tag on grace, who abuse their power and connection to sacred spaces, who twist the emotions and resources of those who seek you. Thank you for showing us how anger can be holy and how we have missed the point because of our great devotion to money.

READER 3: (Read Mark 12:41-44.)

The widow, having lost and given such a tremendous amount, teaches us that there is a difference between giving out of our surplus and giving out of our need. Her offering to you, Jesus, reminds us of the freedom, trust, and interdependency found when we have nothing left to lose and therefore everything else to gain. Let her connection to you illuminate for us how you will always be found in the hungry, thirsty, naked, and imprisoned. That we may look to the margins to know God. Thank you for redefining the magnitude of an offering, for calling the last first.

READER 4: (Read John 13:23-28.)

You have shown us that in the economy of God to be pressed is not to be crushed; that death of one can lead to life for many; that all things are working together for your good. We have seen this in the lives and deaths of people like Dr. Martin Luther King Jr., Mohandas Gandhi, Caesar Chavez, Rosa Parks, and Nelson Mandela—those who have exemplified that non-violent resistance might annihilate the body, but it only spreads the movement. You knew the pain and loneliness and world-sized weight that was ahead of you, and you entered into it anyway because of your great love for us. You teach us about a backward kingdom where protective and retaliatory violence cannot hold a candle to the enduring and brave love of laying down of one's life for a friend. Thank you for knowing that we would need this truth even and especially today. Make our love greater than our fear that we might absorb rather than perpetuate harm.

READER 5: (Read Mark 14:3-9.)

You welcome our willing hearts, Jesus, when those who believe themselves to be closest to you are quick to judge us and keep us out of the fold. You welcome the willing hearts of those whom we believe should be kept out as well. We tell the story now of the woman whose care for you would be shared throughout the world—remembering that we do not get to shun those whom your kingdom must include. Remembering that love is greater than all our attempts to know right and wrong and to exclude accordingly. Thank you, God, for this woman, her generosity toward you, and her understanding of her worth that allowed her to approach you.

May it teach us to be oil-bringers rather than gatekeepers, to know our worth and the worth of others.

READER 6: (Read Mark 14:17-25.)

ONE: The body of Christ is broken that we and this world may be made whole.

ALL: Thank you for the bread that you share at your open table.

ONE: The cup of the new covenant, poured out as a promise that anything oppressive, violent, evil, fear-driven, or dead is not yet finished.

ALL: Thank you for the wine that you share at your open table.

ONE: The basin of water— the same water that parted for your enslaved people, that calmed at your command, that envelops us in baptism, that sustains us every day. Let it symbolize your invitation to us to be wildly loved and to wildly love our neighbors.

ALL: Thank you for the water that connects us here at your open table.

(Invite participants to partake in Holy Communion and feet washing.)

ONE: May you spend the rest of the day considering how Jesus connects with us on Thursday and what he faces for us on Friday.

May you hear your commission: Love as you have been radically loved, though it may mean pain and death.

And take heart. Because this is not the end. Go in peace.

One Body and One Spirit: A Litany for Celebrating a Spectrum of Abilities

Elrena Evans

Parenting a child with invisible disabilities can be hard. Because my middle son looks "normal" (as we've been repeatedly told), when he fails to act "normal," people don't see that he is not a typically developing child. Suffice it to say, my husband and I have been on the receiving end of a lot of assumptions that we are bad parents.

Too many instances of being judged for behaviors I cannot control have rendered me hyper-vigilant about how my son acts, particularly in church. Having been a member of my congregation for over three decades, I long for my son to feel the same love and sense of belonging that I do among our community of believers. And I often feel that if only I could normalize his behavior, then that love and acceptance would be his.

In other churches, where we don't have the investment of decades of relationship, I find it much easier not to care how his behaviors are perceived. I find myself shrugging my shoulders and thinking to myself, *Not my church!* My son wants to lie on his back with his feet in the air? Disappear under the pew and resurface elsewhere? Test out his rendition of the "Worm" during a sermon? Roll in the aisles, literally, making fffffffftt noises? I shrug my shoulders. *Not my church!*

My husband, son, and I were nearing the end of a Sunday-night service in a church we were visiting when the woman in the pew in front of us turned around. I knew what was coming; my son had been flopping and fffffffftt-ing nonstop for the past hour and a half, so I was on the defensive before she even spoke. And when she did, I was ready.

"I am *so glad* you came to church today," the woman said, looking straight at my son.

That was not what I expected to hear.

"It was such a privilege to sit with you," she went on. "I hope you come again!"

A privilege? To sit next to the kid who was practicing the "Worm" and who spent the entire sermon going ffffffftt?

Unsure how to respond, I wondered at first if she was being sarcastic. But she kept talking, telling us about the church cookout and inviting us to come. "Would your son want a hamburger?" she asked. As it turned out, my son did want a hamburger. So we stayed for the church cookout.

That evening, where I expected judgment, I was met with radical welcome. Where I was judgmental myself, I saw God's delight in my child. And I realized this church that was *not my church* was, in fact, a part of my church— because the church is where God's people welcome everyone with God's love.

ONE: God our Creator, we celebrate the beauty and diversity of your children.
ALL: God, we celebrate.

ONE: God our Sustainer, we rejoice in the myriad of ways you have made us unique.
ALL: God, we rejoice.

ONE: God our Redeemer, we thank you that you have called us all to live in relationship with you.
ALL: God, we thank you.

ONE: God of endless paradox, we confess that too often we have chosen predictability, order, and comfort in our worship instead of extending your radical welcome to others.
ALL: Lord, we confess.

ONE: We confess that we long to see your face in the able-bodied, the typical, the beautiful, and the powerful instead of those whom we label "disabled."
ALL: Lord, we confess.

ONE: We confess that what we call inclusion too often is, in fact, tokenism. We repent of having used your people as props for making ourselves feel better.
ALL: Lord, we confess.

ONE: Forgive us for idolizing able-bodiedness and what we perceive as "normal" as if these descriptors are hallmarks of holiness. Forgive us for pursuing sameness instead of godliness.
ALL: God, forgive us.

ONE: Forgive us for believing and acting as if being a "good Christian" means being able to sit still and maintain eye contact.
ALL: God, forgive us.

ONE: Forgive us for not seeing reflections of your beauty in every facet of difference.
ALL: God, forgive us.

ONE: Teach us to love as you love, God. In your holy name we pray:
ALL: Our Father who art in heaven,
Hallowed be thy name.
Thy kingdom come.
Thy will be done
on earth as it is in heaven.
Give us this day our daily bread,
and forgive us our trespasses,
as we forgive those who trespass against us,
and lead us not into temptation,
but deliver us from evil.
For thine is the kingdom,
and the power, and the glory,
for ever and ever.
Amen.

Justice in the Ordinary: A Litany for the Small and Large Decisions of Our Day-to-Day

Cat Caya

When I wake in the morning, I revel in the blessed, bleary moments before the world starts to come into focus. Still in the perceived safety of my bed, I try not to reach for my phone and check the news. I already know what it will show me: stories of death, destruction, hate, and greed. At some point, I have to get up. As I put on my glasses and think about the tasks of the day, I remember that these sad stories are not just happening somewhere else or to someone else—they are close. They are the stories of my neighbors and my community. The weight of all that is broken settles upon me.

God, how can we move with this weight crushing us?

It is easy to think that our own power or influence are not enough to confront the injustices around us, to dismantle systems created to exploit the vulnerable, to bridge the deepening divisions among family and church and country. But there are hundreds of decisions we are presented with every single day that give us the opportunity to show up anyway. Even if an act cannot right an injustice, it is an offering redolent of hope-filled love we can give to a hurting world.

We can show up in small ways. My church strives to be a community that embodies our motto, *Safe to Belong*, something that feels increasingly rare these days. We serve Communion every Sunday to anyone who wants to come to the table. I once presented the bread to an older man wearing a shirt that promoted something I stood firmly against. Still, we looked each other in the eyes, and I handed him the bread. I told him, "This is Christ's body, broken for you." It was an intimate moment that challenged the narrative of *us and them*.

Sometimes, we are called to show up in larger ways. After the violence in Charlottesville, Virginia, in August 2017, I felt shattered. The most healing thing I could think of was to reach for others who felt the same way. We collectively expressed our grief by gathering on a sidewalk, holding signs that read, "Love thy neighbor" and "No hate." We were people of different ages, faiths, and backgrounds, and our sacred lament built bridges between us.

We need to shake ourselves free from the overwhelm of creation's groaning. We cannot be resigned to it, nor the belief that nothing we do can change things. We must offer redemptive love in how we live our lives in the everyday.

ONE: Just and loving God,
Our hearts ache over what is broken.
A holy anger sparks and burns in our chests.
We refuse to give way to cynicism and despair.
ALL: We will call forth shalom.

ONE: May we see the resources we have as plenty:
Clothing, food, supplies, money, time.
Let us see how these resources can be shared.
ALL: We will be generous and giving.

ONE: Contemptuous words come up at the dinner table,
On the street, in the supermarket, at work.
May we not comply to hatred with our silence.
ALL: We will respond with wisdom and grace.

ONE: We want our children to have a better world.
They will learn to speak truth and see humanity
So they can be peacemakers and prophets and healers.
ALL: We will raise them to love.

ONE: When the authorities and systems of the land
Prey on the weak and demonize the different,
When they peddle fear and use it for power,
ALL: We will gather and raise our voices.

ONE: Precious in your eyes are the sons and daughters
Whose lives were taken because of skin color,
Sexual orientation, gender, religion, politics.
ALL: We will say their names and remember.

ONE: Many of our siblings suffer in silence
Because they fear their stories will not be believed.

We declare that their voices matter.
ALL: We will listen to their stories.

ONE: Let there be a table instead of walls.
A seat for the widow, the orphan, the foreigner,
And even a seat for my enemy.
ALL: We will make space for one another.

ONE: The groaning does not stop, and the headlines bleed.
It makes us weary, and we cry out and weep.
While we strive not to let discouragement take over,
ALL: We will not look away.

ONE: We choose acts of life instead of death,
Expressions of mercy and radical faith in the *and yet*,
Believing in the restoration of all things.
ALL: We will show up with hope. Amen.

We Will Laugh, We Will Cry: A Litany for Looking Longer at Pain and Committing to Celebration

Sharifa Stevens

There's a photo depicting a quiet moment amid the violent aftereffects of armed conflict in the Gaza Strip. In what was once a bathroom, now robbed of walls, a father bent by an intact bathtub to bathe his children. The violent exposure of wrecked safety hung in the air of that scene. Also almost tangible was the father's tenderness in his daily task and the slippery joy of the littles. *How are they not huddled in a corner, screaming,* I thought to myself. *How does laughter exist in that shell of a room?*

The trials of pain are midwives to profound depth in both faith and joy. Pain is not something to be celebrated—when humanity and God finally dwell together in uninterrupted glory, pain will be abolished. Yet reckoning with pain, acknowledging it, and persevering through it births humility, compassion, sober-mindedness, tenderness. Like a strict yet dutiful teacher, pain imparts important theological lessons: Death is not God's ideal for us. This is not the end. To get along in the in-between, we need to lean on God and on one another.

Surrounded by the debris of a fallen world, we are still gently doted on by a God who loves us—and that itself is cause for celebration. Hope and faith dwell in the confident swell of the in-spite-of kind of joy. Believing in God is a declaration of dependence—a rebellion against the principalities and powers, a rage against death itself. In a bedeviled world, that declaration sometimes looks like a swell of raucous laughter, an electric slide, a broken piñata showering sweet treats. Or a giggly splash of soap bubbles in a room with no walls.

ONE: As our parents' final breaths draw sobs and sighs, remember
ALL: Jesus is near to us in our tears of grief.

ONE: As we touch our bellies, calling to mind babies born straight into God's arms, remember
ALL: Jesus is the man of sorrows. He understands our pain.

ONE: As our bodies contort with illness, and the diagnosis is grim, remember
ALL: They stretched Jesus wide and hung him high. He felt the pain with us.

ONE: When the refugees flee, displaced, remember
ALL: Jesus left heaven, fled to Egypt, lived under Roman rule. He carries our longing for home.

ONE: When the violence of the age seems stronger than the peace that passes understanding, remember
ALL: There's a cross for us to bear before the glory comes.

ONE: Pain sounds the alarm:
ALL: This is not our home.

ONE: Let the pain wake us to truth:
ALL: This is not the end.

ONE: Look pain in the eye and say, "We feel your grip now,
ALL: But you cannot snatch us from our good God's hand."

ONE: Look pain in the eye and say, "If you insist on walking with us,
ALL: Know we have a rod and staff of comfort from our good Shepherd."

ONE: Look pain in the eye and say, "See the table set before us, the oil of gladness poured over us,
ALL: Watch us dance, watch us sing, watch us live exceedingly, abundantly, eventually. It's coming."

ONE: Look pain in the eye and say,
ALL: "We know the end. God wins."

ONE: Look pain in the eye and celebrate anyway. In rebellion against the empires that oppress,
ALL: We rejoice before the Lord our God.

ONE: In spite of the frailness of our bodies,
ALL: We rejoice before the Lord our God.

ONE: To defy the pain in front of us and the cynicism within us,
ALL: We rejoice before the Lord our God.

ONE: Because there is a Redeemer,
ALL: We rejoice before the Lord our God. Amen.

Looking Inward and Forward: Advent and Lenten Litanies for Peacemakers

Kayla Craig

For Advent

During Advent, we anticipate a new reality. We wait with wonder for the moment heaven meets earth with a holy kiss, changing the course of history forever. With the radical arrival of God in the form of an infant, we stand in the eternal reverberations of a living God who subverts notions of power, redefining love along the way.

As we gather to pray, we reflect on young Mary's words to her graying cousin Elizabeth. We ask, like the poor servant girl, that our souls would glorify the Lord. We gather to rejoice in our Savior, who created an upside-down kingdom that is all at once perfect and holy and nothing we'd ever expect.

In our posture of eager anticipation, we believe this time of expectancy will act as a holy antidote to the spiritual amnesia we're prone to develop. In our remembering, we're spurred to look inward at what is and forward at what is to come. We remember that God has performed mighty deeds, brought down rulers, and lifted the humble—and will continue to do so. We dwell in this kingdom whose merciful King fills the hungry and sends the rich away. We wait, we respond, and we enter into the swirling cosmos of love everlasting, a story that culminates—yet just begins—with a baby born on the margins.

We offer our words as a meditation on the great things the Mighty One has done, is doing, and will do. May God's name be praised.

ONE: In the footsteps of the unwed mother, may we walk in expectant hope.
ALL: Lord, help us journey together, for you are present in the wait. Emmanuel, God with us.

ONE: In the flutters of the old woman, may we rejoice with holy anticipation.

ALL: Lord, help us dance for what is to come, for joy in weary bones is a holy resistance.
Emmanuel, God with us.

ONE: In the closed doors of Bethlehem may we make room for the stranger.
ALL: Lord, help us welcome the weary, for we are fellow sojourners.
Emmanuel, God with us.

ONE: In the tears of the laboring girl, may we be hopeful in our suffering.
ALL: Lord, help us seek refuge in a compassionate God, for the Word has been made flesh.
Emmanuel, God with us.

ONE: In the presence of the midwife, may we sit with others in their pain.
ALL: Lord, help us make space for one another, for as we gather we dwell in sacred community.
Emmanuel, God with us.

ONE: In the commitment of the ordinary carpenter, may we choose to love those whom others deem unworthy.
ALL: Lord, help us hear your voice above all else, for we seek your strength to go against the grain.
Emmanuel, God with us.

ONE: In the arrival of the newborn king, may we experience life abundant.
ALL: Lord, help us live in your upside-down kingdom, for you've ushered in new life.
Emmanuel, God with us.

ONE: In the warmth of the worn cloth, may we wrap our arms around the vulnerable.
ALL: Lord, help us clothe the naked and feed the hungry, for what we do for the least of these, we do unto you.
Emmanuel, God with us.

ONE: In the light of the brilliant star, may we illuminate the shadows cast by fear and hate.
ALL: Lord, help us follow your perfect love, for when we lay our fear at your feet, we are free.
Emmanuel, God with us.

ONE: In the willingness of the dirty shepherds, may we proclaim a gospel of peace for all.

ALL: Lord, help us listen to the poor and powerless, for you choose your messengers in perfect, unexpected ways.

Emmanuel, God with us.

ONE: Amid the jealousy of the angry ruler, may we subvert the powers of the world.

ALL: Lord, help us avoid the empire's allure, for your glorious ways move beyond our idols.

Emmanuel, God with us.

ONE: In the song of the heavenly host, may we hear Jesus in the voices of the unheard.

ALL: Lord, help us awaken to the mystery, for the melodies of your grace linger still.

Emmanuel, God with us.

ONE: In the wisdom of the temple prophetess, may we bear witness in wondrous celebration.

ALL: Lord, help us choose the way of peace, for yours is the kingdom, now and forever.

Amen.

For Lent

During Lent, the church observes and reflects upon the forty days Jesus spent in the wilderness. It was there that he faced great temptation and there that he fasted and prayed. Jesus intimately knows the suffering and the ache of the flesh, and as we observe Lent, we sit in the tension of now and not yet, asking the Lord to help us follow his example to seek God as the Sustainer of all. We gather together to lament and confess the ways we have fallen into temptation. And we ask an ever-merciful God to help us escape these entrapments and entanglements of the soul.

ONE: Help us resist the allure of fear. We have shut our hearts and siloed ourselves, building fences and locking ourselves away.

ALL: For in temptation's snare, we have knelt at the altar of safety.
Christ, have mercy.

ONE: Help us resist the pull of power. We have fallen prey to status and con-
trol, posturing ourselves over our neighbors.
ALL: For in temptation's snare, we have inflated our egos above all.
Christ, have mercy.

ONE: Help us resist the appeal of complacency. We have stayed silent in the
face of oppression, choosing false unity over humanity.
ALL: For in temptation's snare, we have disobeyed your truth and justice.
Christ, have mercy.

ONE: Help us resist the call of violence. We have spat words and spilled
blood, creating enemies and elevating ourselves.
ALL: For in temptation's snare, we have lost the peace of the Lamb.
Christ, have mercy.

ONE: Help us resist the rapture of greed. We have sung hymns of insatiable
want, worshiping our bank accounts.
ALL: For in temptation's snare, we have valued our idols at great cost.
Christ, have mercy.

ONE: Help us resist the charm of distraction. We have numbed our hearts
and avoided your call, self-medicating and succumbing to gluttony.
ALL: For in temptation's snare, we have avoided the calm of your Spirit.
Christ, have mercy.

ONE: Help us resist the overture of anger. We have shouted and screamed,
blasting our opinions like fire hoses.
ALL: For in temptation's snare, we have quenched your gentle Spirit.
Christ, have mercy.

ONE: Help us resist the draw to lethargy. We have insured ourselves out of
pain, hiding under blankets of false comfort.
ALL: For in temptation's snare, we have slept through your call to love.
Christ, have mercy.

ONE: We seek your help in times of temptation. We have turned our face
from you, slipping into the seduction of the serpent.
ALL: For in our broken condition, we have fallen into death's grasp.
Christ, have mercy.

ONE: But we hold onto hope and submit to you
**ALL: Our misplaced fear and power and complacency,
Our misplaced violence and greed and distraction,
Our misplaced anger and lethargy and dismissal.
Christ, have mercy.**

ONE: We lament, O Lord.
ALL: We repent, O Lord.

ONE: We ask for your Spirit to intercede.
ALL: We ask for a guide in the wilderness.

ONE: We turn our face from temptation
ALL: And look instead to the heavens,

ONE: Holding firm to your promise
ALL: That death has conquered death.

ONE: And in your mercy, we are not rendered weak in our inequities;
ALL: But in your Son, we are made whole. Amen.

Racial Reconciliation and Repair: A Litany Toward Just Relationships

Tamara Gurley

As the church, we love and long for the work of repair. We see this redemptive theme written throughout our Bibles, preached from our pulpits, and carried by our voices in worship. The story and work of Jesus is about repair. It's about taking what was once whole—now broken—and bringing it back together again. The work of repair is not accomplished in our sorrow, our shame, our guilt, or our regret. The work of repair is only accomplished in our confession and repentance. By God's grace, we can confess and turn from the ways in which we have harmed one another and, therefore, return to the One who has made right all that has been wrong.

Once we offer confession and repentance, we can then work toward repair. Jesus reconciled the sin of the world through his death and resurrection—first the breaking, then the healing. We must follow this same pattern. We cannot work to mend broken relationships without acknowledging that for which our Savior shed his blood. For we cannot repent of sin we do not acknowledge, and we cannot acknowledge what we do not name. In the work of racial reconciliation, understanding the relationship between repentance and repair is paramount.

In my journey as a follower of Christ and biracial woman of color, I have been both the wounded and the wounder. I have been both the silenced and the silencer. As the Lord pried open my eyes and prompted me to raise my voice about the urgency of discipling followers of Jesus toward just relationships and the dismantling of unjust systems, I fell victim to the wounding apathy and indifference of the church. I was cast out for my conviction and urged to mask my wounds. I was offered cheap repair without repentance and granted shallow ways to fix but not to heal.

I wrote this litany as a cry of my own heart for mercy, grace, and forgiveness. The words petition us to lay down our power and our privilege for the good of the marginalized. It is a plea for us to see all humans as our neighbors and love them as ourselves. It is a cry to lay down our lives for one another as we work to realize God's kingdom on earth.

Confession

ONE: Where we have not understood, have we ever sought to understand?
Where we have swallowed lies for fear of truth,
Tuned out the cries of those whose eyes have seen the darkness,
And turned our cheek toward those whose lives have felt the sting of oppression,
ALL: Lord, forgive us for our apathy.

ONE: People were in need, and we closed our eyes so as not to see them.
For to see a brother is to acknowledge his humanity,
And to see a sister is to acknowledge her likeness;
A co-ruler, co-creator, co-laborer,
Fashioned by God, for God, and in the image of God.
Where we refused to see God's image in a stranger, an inferior, a foe,
ALL: Lord, forgive us for our pride.

ONE: Where we have denied your worth and been careless with your dignity,
Blaming you for your own oppression,
Judging the slave for not being the master,
But never the master for not freeing the slave;
Where we have neither questioned our miseducation
Nor welcomed one another's truth,
ALL: Lord, forgive us for hardening our hearts.

ONE: Seeking good for ourselves, we denied our siblings,
Disobeying the command to be their keeper
And keeping for ourselves what we were called to give.
Where we have loved ourselves more than our neighbor,
Loved our power more than offered obedience to our Savior,
ALL: Lord, forgive us for our greed.

ONE: Where you have suffered while we prospered and sat idly by;
Where our power spoke truth to no one,
And our privilege granted selfish gain;
Where we have not laid down our lives
But rather moved further from you, so that we could rise,
ALL: Lord, forgive us for oppressing.

ONE: Where we were silent when you needed us to speak;
Where we were silent when you needed us to raise our voice;

Where we were silent when we had not been silenced.
Our voice had wings while your voice was stolen,
All: Lord, forgive us for our silence.

ONE: Where safety and comfort have been our closest companions;
Where we could not risk disrupting racial blindness by disciplining our eyes
to see;
Our crime was our indifference in the pursuit of our affluence;
Indifference, worse than hatred, not only wounds but kills.
For the price of our life, liberty, and happiness
Is your blood, freedom, and prosperity.
ALL: Lord, forgive us for our sin.

Repentance

ONE: We acknowledge our privilege and power unearned.
We turn away from our apathy and indifference.
ALL: Lord, grant us your forgiveness.

ONE: We confess our sins to one another as we seek healing.
We long for all that has been broken to be made whole.
ALL: Lord, grant us your grace.

ONE: We petition that our hardened hearts no longer be of stone
And our eyes now awakened never again to be closed.
ALL: Lord, grant us your mercy.

Repair

ONE: May your kingdom come and your will be done on earth as it is in
heaven.
May our hearts long for just relationships, and our words work toward healing wounds.
May our actions promote justice and equity and our prayers be for peace and
unity.
ALL: Lord, we repent and commit to making repairs. Amen.

The Truth Will Set Us Free: A Litany of Remembrance

Delonte Harrod

I attended Paul Quinn College, a historically Black college, in Dallas, Texas, that was unapologetically Christian and Black. Every week, students had to attend a chapel service. In those services, Black preachers always engaged in the holy act of remembering through their preaching. They called on us to remember the injustices done to our communities, and they challenged us to remember the work of the Savior. This kind of posture toward the Lord, God's people, and the community has always stuck with me.

When engaging in the work to help white Christians understand the church's role in slavery, I've been amazed at how some have little knowledge of the history or have chosen to erase the white churches' participation from their memories. Most white Christians in America don't want to remember such atrocities. They think that Black Christians are trying to heap condemnation upon them. Nothing could be further from the truth. Remembering is what we are called to do. Remembering is a part of our calling. We see many instances in the Bible of people being called to remember.

"Moses said to the people, 'Remember this day on which you came out of Egypt, out of the house of slavery, because the LORD brought you out from there by strength of hand; no leavened bread shall be eaten'" (Exod. 13:3).

"You meet those who gladly do right, those who remember you in your ways. But you were angry, and we sinned; because you hid yourself we transgressed" (Isa. 64:5).

Moreover, the Lord called us to remember to drink his blood and eat his flesh when we gather. I wanted to write something to show that the God of the Bible remembers. We are called to remember God and God's ways. We are called to remember the harm that we have done to others. But God doesn't want us to remember in order to condemn us—to lock us in a state of self-hate. God calls us to remember so that we can be drawn in, so that we may be healed and freed, so that we may move forward through the pain and not around it. Remembering rightly is a means of grace.

ONE: Lord, you are the eternal God who sits over all the earth.
ALL: You are the God who remembers.

ONE: You are the God who remembered your covenant promise to Abraham.
ALL: You did not forget.

ONE: You are the God who remembered to bless Sarah's womb. And when Hagar and Ishmael were in the desert without food and comfort, you remembered and blessed them.
ALL: You did not forget.

ONE: For you are the God who remembered your covenant people while they were enslaved in Egypt. You heard their cry and rescued them.
ALL: You did not forget.

ONE: Lord, you have made promises to your people.
ALL: And you are the God who remembers.

ONE: Lord, you not only remember your promises toward us. You also remember where we have fallen short.
ALL: Remind us now.

ONE: You remember when your covenant people sinned against you, and some did not make it to the Promised Land.
ALL: Remind us now.

ONE: Lord, you remember and know that sin disconnects us from you, and you call us to remember your work of redemption, so that we will not be turned away from you.
ALL: Remind us now.

ONE: You are the God who remembers, and you call us to remember. You call us to the holy act of remembering. Lord, as your covenant people, we have failed to remember you.
ALL: Have mercy on us.

ONE: Lord, we have failed to remember that our identity is in you and you alone.
ALL: Forgive us.

ONE: Lord, we have failed to remember the presence of your kingdom on earth.
ALL: Make us new, Lord.

ONE: We drink daily from the rocks of affliction—
Racism,
Sexism,
Patriarchy,
And misogyny—
Instead of remembering the rock that nourishes us in the wilderness.
ALL: Lord, be gracious and empower us to forsake all that is not of you.

ONE: Lord, the nation in which we live hates to remember.
And we helped it in its forgetting.
ALL: Lord, help us to be a people who encourage others to remember you.

ONE: Lord, as we remember you and your ways, lead us.
And make us more gracious, humbler, lighter.
**ALL: Then we shall be the people who will remember and shall live.
   Amen.**

When the Unthinkable Happens: A Litany for When We Gather and Weep

Angela Denker

Twenty-four hours after worship on August 13, 2018, a semitrailer truck smashed into an SUV at the intersection where I turn to preach most Sunday mornings. The church's name is Easter, where we "blur the lines between church and community." Here we praise God and serve Communion in a gymnasium where volleyball leagues are held on weekday evenings. Easter is the name for the resurrection, the day when Jesus rose again after death on the cross. Easter is shorthand for hope and improbable dreams and life—even after death. Tragedy was not supposed to happen here, and yet it did. The driver of the SUV was a thirty-three-year-old mother of two from a tranquil suburb of Minneapolis/St. Paul, Minnesota, a place where people often move when they want to start a family and be safe.

I wasn't there that Monday morning when the unthinkable happened. I was thousands of miles away in California, conducting interviews and research for a book I was writing. I later learned that the mother was hospitalized in critical condition. She was my age; I was a mother too. My church wanted to bring new life, and now its corner signified death.

Months later at a staff meeting, we heard a request for prayer for her. The mother in the accident had been put on hospice care in a persistent vegetative state. The end was coming soon. In his grief, spiraling through fear and regret and the immense responsibility of parenting without her, the woman's husband had called us at Easter. He wanted, he said, to have the funeral there, at Easter-by-the-Lake, where we praised God on Sunday and his wife was nearly killed on Monday. He said that having the service there, where she almost died and we dared hope for resurrection anyway, might bring some peace. Besides, we had space for several hundred people. And that many or more would all gather, where the unthinkable happened and we wept together.

ONE: We waited for your presence;
We prayed for your protection;
The unthinkable happened anyway.
ALL: O God, O God, why have you forsaken us?

ONE: It isn't fair; it isn't right.
It never should have happened.
The unthinkable happened anyway.
ALL: O God, O God, why have you forsaken us?

ONE: You left us when we needed you most.
We're left with fear.
We're left with doubt.
The unthinkable left us empty.
ALL: O God, O God, why have you forsaken us?

ONE: We are in pain.
We hurt.
We cry.
ALL: O God, O God, why have you forsaken us?

ONE: We gather together.
We are not alone.
Together we weep.
ALL: O God, O God, help us live.

ONE: We gather together.
We gather at the Cross.
Wipe our tears.
ALL: O God, O God, help us live.

ONE: We gather together.
We gather at the tomb.
Dry our eyes.
ALL: O God, O God, help us live.

ONE: We gather together
That we might walk together,
That we might live together after tragedy.
ALL: O God, O God, carry us home.

ONE: We gather together.
Could new life be possible
Even when we are surrounded by death?
ALL: O God, O God, resurrect.
Please, O God, resurrect us. Amen.

Renewal: A Repentant, Hopeful Litany for a Changing Church

Sandra Maria Van Opstal

Murals painted along the walls and halls of a community tell us its story. Their images communicate the experiences, identity, and hopes of the people living in their midst. Those of us who live in communities filled with hurting families, relocated migrants, young people gunning one another down often look to those murals to remind us of the beauty that's already here and the beauty that could be. A theological reality that is and has not yet come in its fullness.

Scripture gives us images as well. In Revelation 21, we see the picture of the new heaven and the new earth. This renewal of all things is a reality that has come, but not yet. Or as I like to call it, the *yes but not so much*. There is still death, crying, and mourning. There are still so many tears. The new has come and is coming, but it is not fully here. We believe that things are new; but experientially, we know things are not.

This can be especially pronounced in and through the church, which is often complicit in the pain. Our indigenous brothers and sisters mourn the history of violence from the church. The church in the Middle East is in pain. Our sisters caravan, fleeing from violence, only to be turned away at our borders. Mothers are losing their babies to gun violence, and churches do nothing but blame the youth. There are tears! The new has come, but not so much!

God is making all things new. Until that day, our worship is more than praying and singing. Worship is formation because the practices we participate in shape us. What might it look like for us to stand with people in prayer and worship? To pray prayers for the whole church as well as the needs of others? To confess our complicity in the injustice in the world and to repent and change? To mobilize others toward repentance and the work of compassion and justice?

Like a mural, the church tells a story through its words, actions, and values. We are an image to the people who will never pick up a Bible. We could be a foretaste of heaven, a pointer to the new heaven and earth. We help people to see the nature of who God is and what God's about when we stand with one another in worship and solidarity. We are heaven on earth. We have assurance that in the end God will reconcile all things to God's self, all wrong things will be made right. We point to the coming kingdom with our actions and lives. We confess together, repent together, and hope together for a church that has been transformed and is being changed.

———————

ONE: Lord, you have shown us your ways of compassion and justice.
Forgive us for being so caught up in our own lives.
Forgive us for not having eyes to see and closing them when we don't want to see.
Forgive us for not having ears to hear and covering them when we don't want to hear.
Forgive us for not knowing you, seeking you, and following you.
ALL: Revive your church. Renew us and remake us in your image.
Revive your church. Renew us so that we may point others to a new heaven and a new earth.

ONE: Jesus, you modeled sacrifice and love for neighbor.
Deliver us from our anemic and self-focused faith practices.
Deliver us from narcissism in our worship practices that center on us and not others.
Deliver us from fear that keeps us from taking risks in order to serve our neighbor.
Deliver us from apathy in our own hearts toward those at the margins.
ALL: Revive your church. Renew us and remake us in your image.
Revive your church. Renew us so that we may point others to a new heaven and a new earth.

ONE: Holy Spirit, you promise to root, strengthen, and guide us.
Fill us with courage to speak out and speak up when we feel weak.
Fill us with assurance that you are working in ways we can't always see.
Fill us with power to act and love and be the church you are making us to be.
Fill us with the wisdom of a gentle dove and a shrewd serpent that we may be effective.
ALL: Revive your church. Renew us and remake us in your image.
Revive your church. Renew us so that we may point others to a new heaven and a new earth.

ONE: Lord, you promised that you are coming back in your fullness to restore and renew.

Help us to be made new now and at your full return.

Help us to confess together, repent together, and hope together for the church.

Help us to live into the reality that we serve a God who will make wrong things right.

Help us point to the coming kingdom with our actions and lives.

ALL: Revive your church. Renew us and remake us in your image.

Revive your church. Renew us so that we may point others to a new heaven and a new earth.

The Squeaky Wheel: A Litany for Being Close in Proximity to and Advocating on Behalf of One's Neighbor

D. L. Mayfield

I live in a neighborhood that is sometimes described as under-resourced: "failing" public schools, pawn shops, and fast-food restaurants abound, but no public parks or community centers can be found. It's a lower-income suburb in the first stages of gentrification, with rent costs on the rise and a select few trying to cash in on a neighborhood in transition. I like to walk and pray, and I often come away with conflicting thoughts: The systems and structures of my neighborhood are often cruel to the most marginalized, yet my neighbors experiencing poverty bring a brightness and vibrancy that will be lost once they are displaced.

I used to try and love my neighbors by being kind to them. Now I have discovered that unless I start speaking up and advocating for real life issues like renters' rights, they won't be my neighbors for much longer. Here is a litany for anyone wanting to pay attention and those resolving to get involved or stay present in justice work.

ONE: Jesus told them a parable about their need to pray always and not to lose heart. He said, "In a certain city there was a judge who neither feared God nor had respect for people. In that city there was a widow who kept coming to him and saying, 'Grant me justice against my opponent.' For a while he refused; but later he said to himself, 'Though I have no fear of God and no respect for anyone, yet because this widow keeps bothering me, I will grant her justice, so that she may not wear me out by continually coming.' And the Lord said, 'Listen to what the unjust judge says. And will not God grant justice to his chosen ones who cry to him day and night? Will he delay long in helping them? I tell you, he will quickly grant justice to them.'"*

ALL: God of love, let us rest in our belovedness.

ONE: When we walk our neighborhoods, help us pay attention to the birds of the air and to the beauty of the flowers. To the ways the seasons change or don't, to the ways our neighborhoods change the longer we stay. Let us see the ways people dress in certain times, the smells coming from houses and apartments, the shops and stores, the developments moving in. Help us pay attention to who is thriving and who is not. Who is being invested in, and who has been systematically shut out? Who owns the land? Who gets the deals to develop? Who profits off of progress? Who sends their kids to the local school, and who does not? Who has options? Who is stuck in the middle of surviving?

Let us be troubled in our neighborhoods; let us be troubled in our lives. Help us be grateful for the beauty and help us not accept the inequality that can be found underneath nearly every surface. Let us pay attention to the cruelty of a system that values capital over people. Let us see the ones you love who have been left behind in the race to achieve the American Dream.

ALL: God of love, let us rest in the belovedness of our neighbors.

ONE: Let us not close our eyes, even—especially—when we want to. Let us notice what is closest to us, let it trouble us until we cannot help but speak out. Let us send emails to city council members on issues that affect the most marginalized. Let us pull aside our pastor for a few words on inclusivity, on recognizing the range of experiences and trauma within a congregation. Let us comment on the Facebook posts we see that dehumanize. Let us schedule meetings with developers and ask who will benefit from all of this progress. Let us always be thinking about who is not represented, who ultimately will pay the price for our decisions, policies, theologies. Let us firmly, consistently, and with great love raise our hands and ask questions with a slightly shaky voice. Let us disrupt the cycles of power and affluence and autonomy with a singular, insistent focus. May we ask ourselves, *Who are our neighbors, and who isn't flourishing?* How can we advocate for their shalom?

ALL: God of love, let us rest in our belovedness.

ONE: Give us grace to experience the pushback of people unused to being confronted with uncomfortable realities. Let us accept the title of divisive. Let us be difficult people to the ones whose lives are built by capitalizing on the disinvestment of others.

Help us to love even those who are threatened by our consistent questions.
Help us resist the temptation to numb out, to despair, to go silent in the
face of our own complicity or corruption or ineffectiveness.

Remind us that there are unjust judges in the world who need persistent
widows in order to change. Give us, your beloved people, the stamina to
keep knocking on the doors of power, confident that our current reality
is not your dream for the world.

Help us pray with our lives, our hands, our feet, our eyes. Help us pay attention. Help us keep speaking up, proclaiming that all is not well if it is only
well for some. And let us find a glimpse of your justice in our lives and in
our communities and wherever we can.

ALL: Lord, hear our prayers. Amen.

*Luke 18:1-8

A Lament for an Unrelenting Earth

Patrice Gopo

Some days I wake in the morning disoriented, my mind mixing up my dreamscape with the reality of what transpires in life. In my dreamscape, my arms reach for a perfect cerulean sky. This image becomes the metaphor for the total goodness and beauty I wish would enfold this earth we inhabit. Then I awaken in full to a new day with the weight of all that remains unchanged pressing against my shoulders and telling me to keep my eyes closed. Sometimes I want to keep my eyes closed so that I can continue imagining a different sort of world—a world empty of natural disasters, empty of human beings holding hateful intent toward other human beings.

One such week, full of these terrible events, prompted the words of lament unfolding in this litany. I hesitate to name the week because I find these events could be part of another week or another week or another week. But I wrote these words as a yearning to encounter hope even as I experienced a depth of hopelessness. I wrote these words because although this earth can be unrelenting, I wanted a space to acknowledge and confess the ways we are complicit. I wrote these words because I wanted to remember that *unrelenting* can also describe God.

ONE: This earth we inhabit is a place
Where hurricanes ravage and mudslides refuse to retreat,
Where hate carries torches instead of cowering in fear,
Where too often we speak of lives lost as numbers and not names,
Where our place of birth impacts our length of life.
ALL: Our children sing of a world held in your hands.
The psalmist writes of righteousness and justice, the foundations of your throne.

ONE: In Lamentations, we read of your mercies.
Your mercies, O Lord, are new every morning.
But what happens when the foundations of righteousness and justice

Become rubble beneath our bare feet?

ALL: When we wake in the morning and the new day is worse than the old,
When we don't see the righting of wrongs,
When we don't find you in the groan of the wind,
In the splintering of quaking land,
In the heat of flames and fire.

ONE: Instead, all we hear is a whisper: a still small voice.
But, Lord, we don't want just whispers.
We long for the might of raging rivers that carve canyons,
Of hands raised that calm the storm,
Of a light that defeats the darkness.
ALL: We cry out, "Show us the foundations of your throne!"

ONE: And you, Lord, invite us forth into a sacred confession that gives rest.
Make us people who can say, "We confess there are ways we have kneeled before a power that ignores instead of falling face down at the foot of the cross."
"We confess that we are complicit in maintaining the very world we say we want changed."
ALL: "We confess we have thirsted at the fount of a comfort that blinds."

ONE: With these words of confession, we say for ourselves and our communities,
ALL: Holy, holy, holy Lord God Almighty!

ONE: The very foundation of all that was and is and is to come,
You hold this spinning planet between your holy palms.
This earth is held, this earth is held, this earth is held.
If your mercies are new each day, O Lord, then as the earth spins on its axis
And faces the rising sun,
ALL: Make us fearless beacons of your radiant light. Amen.

Sacred Vessels of the Holy: A Litany for Honoring the Bodies (Minds, Hearts, and Souls) of Women

Elaina Ramsey

The most spirit-filled moments for me often happen not in church but in unlikely spaces. Among ordinary people and settings. Among those most misunderstood. One such instance occurred when I served as a panelist for a reproductive justice conference where a colleague asked everyone to snap their fingers if they ever experienced or knew someone who had endured sexual harassment, violence, or abuse. Without hesitation, the room full of hundreds of activists echoed with snaps of affirmation.

Once again, in call-and-response form, the speaker asked us to snap our fingers if those same mistreated individuals ever received *justice* to ease their pain. Aching silence filled the room.

As a rape survivor who advocates for bodily autonomy (including abortion access), I know that deafening silence all too well. It haunts and cripples me on the worst of days. But in that moment and in that room, I was filled with a fire for justice and a sense of kinship with all the women who dwelled there. We saw one another. We heard one another's pain. And we were believed. How miraculous that women persist day after day through such adversity. How astounding that we rise above the countless lies that try to make us less than.

In the Bible—and beyond—fibs and falsehoods abound that portray women as tempters and seducers. Faulty teachings flourish that view women as submissive helpmates to ornament and serve men without question. Untruths prosper, holding women captive to impossible standards of beauty, caregiving, and perfection. Deceitful practices thrive that seek to control and legislate women's bodies, choices, and reproductive lives. How curious then that Jesus would be born of a poor, Brown, unwed girl who magnified the Lord with her very body, with her sacred choice and consent. How divinely subversive that the gospel centers on the very testimony of Mary Magdalene

163

and other women. Yet, these very first witnesses of the resurrection were not believed, since the disciples viewed their words as an "idle tale" (Luke 24:11).

For all the women who long to be seen, heard, and believed, this litany is for us. As deep calls unto deep, I pray these words wash over us with abundant assurance and truth. These words are for the wondrous, the weary, the wounded. May we rise up and reclaim our power. May we heal and extend hope. May we proclaim truth and break the silence.

In times of triumph or dismay and everywhere in between, may we sit in the stillness and bask in the brilliance of all that we are. In times of doubt and despair, may our community find the courage to hold our pain—and to honor our strength. And in the most unlikely moments and places, may we encounter brave souls willing to fight like holy hell with us to bring forth the kin-dom of God.

In the depths of our being, may we know that we are beloved. We are of sacred worth.

ONE: For the battered, bruised, and broken,
For all who bear assaults to their dignity—mind, body, and soul,
For all who have been discredited and dismissed,
ALL: Deep calls unto deep. We see you. We hear you. We believe you.

ONE: For our immigrant kin who face discrimination and threats of family separation,
For our Muslim kin who are misunderstood and maligned in unspeakable ways,
For our indigenous kin whose land, cultures, and bodies are exploited time and again,
ALL: Deep calls unto deep. We see you. We hear you. We believe you.

ONE: For our Latinx and Asian sisters who are rendered invisible by white supremacy,
For our queer, femme, and trans sisters who are erased and excluded with every passing breath,
For our Black sisters who are forced to survive among those enslaved by ignorance and hate,
ALL: Deep calls unto deep. We see you. We hear you. We believe you.

ONE: For the single mothers and working women in all their labors,
For all those who long to bear children and those who do not,

For the lonely, the anxious, and the caregivers among us,
ALL: Deep calls unto deep. We see you. We hear you. We believe you.

ONE: As deep calls unto deep, may you arise in all of your giftedness and
   glory.
As deep calls unto deep, may you move in this world with power and grace.
As deep calls unto deep, may you live as a holy vessel of love, fully knowing,
ALL: You are beloved. You are of sacred worth.

ONE: In the spirit of our ancestors and foremothers, remember who you are
   and whose you are.
In the spirit of the Creator who calls you image-bearer of the Divine,
In the spirit of the *sheroes* of the faith and the Light within you,
ALL: You are beloved. You are of sacred worth.

ONE: As deep calls unto deep, we see you.
As deep calls unto deep, we hear you.
As deep calls unto deep, we believe you.
ALL: You are beloved. You are of sacred worth. Amen.

As It Is in Heaven: A Protest Litany for When We March, Sing, Make Art, Prepare for Nonviolent Civil Disobedience, and Pray on Behalf of a Backward Kingdom

AnaYelsi Velasco-Sanchez

One of the most beautiful things about returning to scripture and learning to read it through a decolonized (one that has deconstructed the dominating Christianity of colonization) lens is the way in which it reinvigorates the Creator's word. For some of us, these are stories that we have read time and time again and, by virtue of their familiarity, they have lost some of their luster. In my journey to reconcile who I am as a woman of color with who I am as a Christian, I've been afforded the gift of seeing things in a new light. This offers comfort, healing, and liberation. It's through this decolonized lens that I returned to the story of the building of the tabernacle in Exodus 35. As Moses is directing the people of Israel in the building of the tabernacle, we are offered a guide for all movement toward justice.

> Let whoever is of a generous heart bring the LORD's offering: gold, silver, and bronze . . . All who are skillful among you shall come and make all that the LORD has commanded . . . And they came, everyone whose heart was stirred, and everyone whose spirit was willing, and brought the LORD's offering to be used for the tent of meeting, and for all its service, and for the sacred vestments. So they came, both men and women; all who were of a willing heart brought brooches and earrings and signet rings and pendants, all sorts of gold objects, everyone bringing an offering of gold to the LORD. And everyone who possessed blue or purple or crimson yarn or fine linen or goats' hair or tanned rams' skins or fine leather, brought them. Everyone who could make an offering of silver or bronze brought it as the LORD's offering; and everyone who possessed acacia wood of any use in the work, brought it. All the skillful women spun with their hands, and

brought what they had spun in blue and purple and crimson yarns and fine linens. (Exod. 35:5-25)

We are so often inclined to create hierarchy. Even in justice work, we revert back to this need to rank the necessity and value of each person's role. We ask ourselves, *Am I doing enough? risking enough? Are my contributions relegated to the background or found on the front lines?*

Nothing lasting can be built with a few skilled workers. We require the benefactors, the craftspeople, the engravers, the designers, the embroiderers, and the weavers. Our strength is in our capacity to counsel, sharpen, and support one another.

ONE: Our God is an incomparable creator, storyteller, healer, and intercessor. God's artistry can be seen from thunderous skies to sun-kissed skin. Made in God's image, we bear the capacity to reflect all of who God is.

ALL: The Creator has made us to be a people that honor every embodiment of divinity. Let us welcome a spaciousness that allows for each of our gifts. Let us heed one another's guidance.

ONE: We turn to our mourners for a recognition of brokenness, an exposure to the depths of our pain. They remind us of our need for healing, mercy and justice, calling us to feel before we act.

ALL: The Creator has made us to be a people who bear one another's wounds. Let us heed the guidance of our mourners.

ONE: We turn to our prophets for a confrontation of reality, a calling back to what was intended. Their words render us convicted. They leave us tender and welcoming to a change of course.

ALL: The Creator has made us to be a people who are open to God's will. Let us heed the guidance of our prophets.

ONE: We turn to our storytellers for a memory of where we have come from and an understanding of where we desire to go. They offer us something in which to be grounded—a people, a history, an ethos, a vision for the not yet realized.

ALL: The Creator has made us to be a people who require relationship and connection. Let us heed the guidance of our storytellers.

ONE: We turn to our intercessors for fortification and revelation. They teach us how to pursue intimacy with the Holy Spirit and go before us when we cannot go ourselves.

ALL: The Creator has made us to be a people who desire empowerment and counsel. Let us heed the guidance of our intercessors.

ONE: We turn to our artists for inspiration and provocation. They employ shape, color, movement, and expression to stir us out of our complacency.

ALL: The Creator has made us to be a people who respond to imagination. Let us heed the guidance of our artists.

ONE: We turn to our front-liners for an example of what it is to dare—dare to step into the streets, dare to speak truth to power, and dare to place our bodies on the line. They lead us into conflict, reminding us that change does not come without risk and sacrifice.

ALL: The Creator has made us to be a people who stand in the gap, persistent in our demands for what is just. Let us heed the guidance of our front-liners.

ONE: We turn to our pillars in the movement for the support and care that sustains us in our mission. They provide a place to rest our heads, resources to fund the work, encouragement for our spirits, and sustenance for our bodies.

ALL: The Creator has made us to be a people who are rich in generosity and hospitality. Let us heed the guidance of our pillars in the movement.

ONE: We turn to our healers for restoration and balance. They allow the Spirit to work through them as a way to pull us back—back from illness and injury, back from grief and pain, back from fear and anger.

ALL: The Creator has made us to be a people who use our bodies, minds, and spirits to mend the bodies of others. Let us heed the guidance of our healers.

ONE: Let us not just pray. Let us not just speak. Let us not just act. Let us remember that we are many parts of a single body moving in a hurting world.

We have been gifted as mourners, prophets, storytellers, intercessors, artists, front-liners, pillars in the movement, and healers so that we may usher creation toward a kin-dom here on earth.

ALL: The Creator has made us to be a people who would rise up with courage and share our gifts for the fulfillment of God's promise. Let us now rise up. Amen.

Repentance for Head-Patters: A Litany for Confessing and Grieving Paternalism in Christian Ministry and Missions

Breanna Randall

Before I moved to southeast Asia, a good deal of folks went out of their way to vigorously encourage me with these words, "You will fall in love with the people!" People who already lived there and were doing Christian service work said similar things, adding that I would develop "a heart for these lost people." This sort of talk troubled me. Why did everyone insist on talking about people in far off places like they were unclaimed puppies at the humane society? It seemed incredibly condescending and even oppressive. Would we talk about our own neighbors or friends that way? Would we discuss people who shared our language, our ethnicity, our socioeconomic status as "lovable" and "lost"? If we did, it would likely be laughable.

I wish I could say that this sort of talk was an anomaly. I wish I could say with confidence that the majority of the cross-cultural relationships between wealthy Christians and the people they intend to "serve" are defined by respect, partnership, and an earnest desire on the part of the wealthy person to understand the life, culture, and struggles of their new friends. I wish I could say that the wealthy Christians I see overseas were deeply uncomfortable taking positions of power over others or that they were even aware that the existing power structures naturally place them in a position over local people that tends toward exploitation. I wish I could say that the majority of world's wealthy, mission-minded Christians were concerned with inequality and injustice.

But most of what I witness appears to be a gauzy, thin love for Jesus, thrown like a cloak over other desires: a thirst for exotic experiences, the thrill of being praised by other Christians, the affirmation of being placed at the top of a spiritual hierarchy. I've observed a dangerous trend of many Western Christians confusing commitment to God with a passion for a system that automatically puts them at the top of the spiritual pecking order. The cost to the people they claim to serve is not insignificant, and it often goes unspoken, lost in translation, lost in the world of manners and courtesy and honor for the outsider, no matter how rude the outsiders' behavior. I grieve these things all the time. I grieve the times my local friends have come to me to talk about Christian missionaries, the times I've had to hear them say, "They don't care about us. They look down on us."

Where I live, touching another adult's head is notoriously rude behavior. Years ago, I read a Lonely Planet guidebook that admonished tourists, saying, "Don't touch anyone on the head." I laughed at the time and promptly reached out to pet my husband's head. But a question remained after the joke was over: Why do travelers need to be admonished thus? (I'm confident that the Lonely Planet guidebooks for Europe don't include such an exhortation.) This piece of travel advice belies a deeper issue: a tendency to look down on and belittle those who don't look, sound, or live like we do and, moreover, to downplay the legitimacy of others' suffering and experiences because they don't match our own.

Much of American Christianity promotes and sustains a culture of head-patters. In this reality, we live with spiritual cataracts. We run over people without noticing what we have done. In our mind's eye, we go into the world bearing all sorts of blessings. Too often we are mistaken. Too often we have confused our own presence with the presence of God; we have preferred our own glory to the goodness of God. We have thought ourselves to be doing good, when in reality we are delivering a curse.

ONE: "Talk no more so very proudly,
let not arrogance come from your mouth;
for the Lord is a God of knowledge,
and by [God] actions are weighed"*
ALL: You are a God who knows. You are a God who sees.

ONE: For where we have failed to love others with the humility and grace
    of Jesus,
Where we have declared that others are darkness and that we are light,
Where we have failed to love people right where they are,
Where we have forced our agendas upon others,
Where we have made it clear to others that we will only love them condition-
    ally, that we will only love them if they accept our message,
ALL: Forgive us, O God. We ask you to restore us.
We ask you to restore the ones who have been hurt.

ONE: For where we've told and shared stories that are not ours to tell,

Where we've listened to exploitative stories without objection,

Where we have failed to ask ourselves how this hurts your world and your beloved,

ALL: Teach us to be better listeners, O God.

Forgive us for loving the sound of our own voices.

Help us to hear the wisdom of your Holy Spirit more clearly.

ONE: For where we have looked down upon others,

Where we have failed to examine our own hearts,

Where we have failed to confront the racism that divides the church,

Where we have failed to confront the racism that poisons the church's witness in the world,

ALL: O God, we ask you to reveal our hidden faults to us.

Show us our tendencies toward racism.

Reveal to us the ways we unwittingly belittle others.

Holy Spirit, help us to see the world with your eyes, with eyes of love.

ONE: For where we have used our influence to pressure others,

Where we have loved our own privilege without considering what it costs others,

Where we have not imitated the humble love of Christ,

ALL: O God, forgive us for our pride.

Forgive us for our hardheartedness, our lack of curiosity, our unwillingness to learn.

ONE: For where we have longed for the praise of people rather than resting in our identity as your beloved,

Where we have taken our loneliness and our insecurities, our desire to be greatest in the kingdom of God and forced the poor and vulnerable to carry the burdens of our spiritual poverty,

Where we have loved the ways that church and ministry give us a sense of superiority,

ALL: O God, forgive us for our thirst for power.

Forgive us for rejecting the commands of Jesus and instead hastily accepting the titles of *teacher* and *pastor*.**

ONE: For where we have loved authority,

Where we have believed ourselves to be saviors, able to replace Christ rather than imitate him,

Where we have used your word as a weapon against others,

Where we have failed to ask questions of those in leadership,

Where we have failed to keep your church accountable for its influence around the globe,

For when others have come to ask us for help, when they have told us about their abuse at the hands of the church, and we have closed our ears,

ALL: O God, forgive us.

You are a God who knows. You are a God who sees.

You are a God of justice for the oppressed, and you will not forget those who suffer.

We confess our complicity, our failure to keep others accountable.

Forgive us for our complacency, O God.

Restore those whom we have injured by what we have done and by what we have left undone. Amen.

*1 Samuel 2:3
**Matthew 23:8

Kind and Compassionate Masculinity: A Litany for Dismantling a Toxic Patriarchy

Juan Carlos Huertas

I still remember the laughter when I got out of the car the first time. I was a fourteen-year-old Puerto Rican in Alexandria, Louisiana. I did not know the language well and certainly did not know the culture. As my father dropped me off for my first day of high school, I did what I had always done as a sign of blessing and respect. I leaned over to kiss my father on the cheek as he kissed mine. Little did I know that this traditional act would be seen as weird and repulsive to my fellow classmates.

That was just the beginning of my initiation into American masculinity. I would soon learn that maleness meant not wearing colorful pants (I still love brightly colored pants) or using a purse (my father, like many other Latin American men, always used one). It meant oversexualization, little emotion, and an emphasis on toughness to the point of violence. It also meant valuing sports over arts, a suspicion of education, and a preference for entertainment over culture.

It was not until my late college years that I began to question the assumptions of American masculinity. A new world was opened to me—a world of philosophy, theology, and sociology about gender, sexuality, and roles in society. I realized that there was nothing wrong with the way that I understood masculinity, that it was good to be different. Then as a religious leader, I began to recognize that I needed to do more than be different; I needed to help others find their understanding.

As a father of two boys, I am more cognizant of the importance of modeling and teaching a nontoxic masculinity and a non-patriarchal way of being in the world. This work is complicated, but I am finding that as I center my life around the Divine, I experience a freedom like never before to be me, to be male, to be open, to be freed. I pray that the rhythms of the ritual life that we are introducing in these pages become our centering mantra as we seek wholeness, healing, and new life, a kind and compassionate way of being male in our homes, neighborhood, cities, and world.

———————

ONE: We confess that we have made you male, and in doing so we have made maleness divine.
ALL: Eternal One, free us!

ONE: We confess that we have made power and control our god and called it your divine will.
ALL: Eternal One, free us!

ONE: We confess that we have believed that male bodies are the only ones made in God's image and that female bodies are made in man's image. These beliefs have defined our relationships to one another in the world.
ALL: Eternal One, free us!

ONE: We confess that we have developed systems that maintain male supremacy.
ALL: Eternal One, free us!

ONE: We confess that we have used "science" as a way to prove that men are superior to women and that white men are superior to men of color. That we have used physiological differences and made them mean weakness, prescribed roles and made them part of natural law, thereby gendering certain human traits.
ALL: Eternal One, free us!

ONE: We confess that we have utilized the Bible with its patriarchy as a weapon against women. We have promoted male headship, which has kept women from being equal partners in the home, the marketplace, and the church. We have used Eve's tale to subjugate women.
ALL: Eternal One, free us!

ONE: We confess that under the disguise of provision, we have robbed women of their agency, have kept them from maximizing their gifts in their communities, and have continued unequal pay in the workplace.
ALL: Eternal One, free us!

ONE: We confess that under the myth of protection, we have excused violence as a sign of maleness, have spread fear to stay in control, and have made women more vulnerable in all aspects of life.
ALL: Eternal One, free us!

ONE: We confess that our views of women as inferior continue to feed our phobias of those in the LGBTQIA+ community. These views hide from us the reality that God's image is in all people, even those whose lives we do not understand.

ALL: Eternal One, free us!

ONE: We confess that because of our cultural patriarchy, we have objectified women in all aspects of life. We have used them to sell, used them to advance, used them to entertain, used them to impress, used them to punish, used them for release.

ALL: Eternal One, free us!

ONE: We confess that the church has often led the way in women's dehumanization, and in doing so we have furthered the physical, emotional, and spiritual trauma that women experience in our world.

ALL: Eternal One, free us!

ONE: Eternal One, may your loving mercy, your steadfast love, and your compassion bring us healing. May you convict us of our idolatry of maleness and help us celebrate the unique ways through which we are called to live in the world. By the power of the Spirit, help us to be faithful partners with our siblings no matter their gender, orientation, or sexual preference. Help us be respectful of one another so that we may hear others' stories. Help us to have courage as we continue to work for a more just world, and help us model a whole way of being male in the world.

ALL: Amen.

Hurts That Hurt: A Litany for Surviving Trauma and Finding Help for Healing

Elaina Ramsey

Sometimes I'm afraid to go to sleep.

One time I dreamt that I took an Uber ride and sat in the front passenger seat, happily holding my purse, which happened to contain the friendliest squirrel. It was a lovely dream that quickly turned into a nightmare when the driver began to grope me. I woke up weeping and wryly thinking that women are more likely to be assaulted than to carry a fuzzy squirrel on their person.

Other times my nightmares terrorize me by taking physical form. As I subconsciously dream of being sexually attacked by shadowy figures, I awaken to my own screams as I blindly defend myself and repeatedly punch my partner in bed. In a shocked stupor, he does his best to calm me down. But the anguish and tears remain as I spiral into guilt over how my past traumas hurt those whom I love. No amount of trigger or content warnings can protect survivors like me from the afflictions of such invasive and wounding dreams. Like others who've experienced trauma, I find myself seeking different forms of pain management—deep breathing, mindfulness, and therapy. But all of these tools can never undo the hurt that dwells within. We are always in recovery.

While trauma is often a lonely journey, the Hebrew Bible reminds me that we are never alone. For seventy years, the people of Israel endured oppression during Babylonian captivity. Yet, in their despair, they were never forsaken by Yahweh. From traumatizing exile to tepid liberation, the Israelites learned to face the future with hope as a community.

For those of us who have survived war, abandonment, cancer, abuse, the loss of a loved one, or generational trauma, this litany is for us. May we know that we're not alone. May we remember that faith, hope, and love endure. And during the moments and seasons when this promise does not seem true, when peace and comfort elude us, when all we want to do is shake our fists and scream into the abyss, when we are unable to face the future with hope, may our communities hold onto hope for us and love us back to life again.

ONE: We gather in stubborn love, seeking to hold space for those whose hurts are deep and often unseen.
ALL: God of hope, comfort your people.

ONE: When sorrow becomes all-consuming and despair threatens to swallow our loved ones whole,
ALL: God of recovery, comfort your people.

ONE: Protect those whose bodies, spirits, and trust have been broken time and time again.
ALL: God of healing, comfort your people.

ONE: Be with those who sleep in fear and who seek shelter in the storm.
ALL: God of hope, comfort your people.

ONE: Strengthen the survivors among us who wrestle with doubt and depression.
ALL: God of recovery, comfort your people.

ONE: Grief upon grief. Tears upon tears. Pain upon pain.
ALL: God of healing, comfort your people. May those who are scarred by struggle be transformed by hope. Amen.

All Shall Be Well: A Closing Prayer for Making It Through Together

Britney Winn Lee

In just a few short months, our world has experienced detrimental wildfires and devastating floods, political trauma and earthquakes after hurricanes after earthquakes. As I write this, I'm quarantined at home in what we can only assume are the beginning days of a global pandemic, the likes of which the world has not yet seen. Good people have died this year, more will follow. Systems have been turned on their heads, and countless communities have stood at the edges of fresh tragedy wondering where to start, how, and if.

But people have also rallied together for the sake of the most vulnerable around them. They have pooled their money, sewn supplies for first responders, come alongside the poor and elderly, and pressed seeds back into the ash of charred soil. They have written messages of love and hope in vibrant chalk on their sidewalks, figured out ways to sing though separated, and put themselves on the front lines for their neighbors. They have marched, voted, painted, baked, held, danced, planted, and started over and over and over again. Their community has become a version of itself that it didn't know it could be before. There is a lot that a moment of impossible suffering can do, but there is so much more that it cannot touch. This final litany reminds us that hope endures; goodness prevails; people surprise us; and love cannot, has not, will not fail. Keep going.

ONE: Everything can change in a moment.
Disaster can take our certainty,
Our plans for the coming months,
The health we thought would be ours,
And the people that made our lives full.
ALL: Lord, have mercy. Christ, have mercy.

ONE: Tragedy can shake the firmest foundation
And consume our homes by flood.
Grief can rob our chests of deep breaths
And our minds of every clear thought.
ALL: Lord, have mercy. Christ, have mercy.

ONE: The darkness can threaten the marginalized,
Who were vulnerable before its coming.
It can bring out the worst in our humanity
And expose the fears that we nurse.
ALL: Lord, have mercy. Christ, have mercy.

ONE: War, disease, disaster, and violence
Can rewrite a story we loved.
Injustice can leave us beyond exhausted.
"How long, O God!" we cry out.
ALL: Lord, have mercy. Christ, have mercy.

ONE: But here's what it cannot do:
It cannot stop the sun from rising
Or grace from being free.
It cannot contain the abundant creativity
That explodes amid limitations.
ALL: Emmanuel, God is with us.

ONE: Loss cannot restrain the helpers
From meeting the needs of neighbors.
Pain will not keep the people from singing
Or the grass from growing again.
ALL: Emmanuel, God is with us.

ONE: Every ounce of chaos couldn't kill the bravery
We learned was inside of us.
And no new normal can steal the memories
That taught us how to love.
ALL: Emmanuel, God is with us.

ONE: This moment, no matter how dark or how long,
Can't make us belong to one another less.
And not one single thing in all of creation
Can separate us from God's love.
ALL: Emmanuel, God is with us.

ONE: All shall be well, love has not failed,
ALL: We'll make it through together.

ONE: All shall be well, love will not fail,
ALL: We'll make it through together.

ONE: All shall be well, love cannot fail,
ALL: We'll make it through together. Amen.

A BENEDICTION FROM THE EDITOR

Go, now, in the light of the Creator,
Who knitted us, our bodies, our vastly deep souls, our complex and diverse
    sexualities, our skin and our voices, our hands and our feet, our hunger
    for beauty and connection and restoration within our mothers' wombs;
Who called the enslaved God's chosen people
And made a home among the oppressed;
Who parted seas that threatened an ending
And brought down walls that blocked a path.
Go, now, in the hope of Christ Jesus,
Who elevated the weak to the strong;
The tradespeople to disciples;
The prostitute to anointer;
The sinner to saint;
Who condemned anyone who would throw stones.
Who said that the downcast, the mourning, and the meek would inherit the
    earth and the kingdom;
Who said that the merciful would receive mercy and the peacemakers would
    be God's children;
Who had enemies and loved them;
Who had enemies and died for them;
Who took on the sins of the world so that we might release our need to be
    the judge;
Who is alive again today.
Go, now, in the power and comfort of the Holy Spirit,
Who hovered over the waters, turning chaos into order;
Who filled the tabernacle and tore the veil and danced in tongues of fire;
Who leads us into the Word of God and leads the Word of God into us;
Who is our dynamic, ever-present counselor and friend;
Who is teaching us still;
Leading us still;
Changing us still;
Meeting us still;
Calling us still into the mysteries of faith
And the full life that is found at our neighbor's side.
Go, now, in peace.

CONTRIBUTORS

Rev. Jeannie Alexander is the director of No Exceptions Prison Collective, an abolitionist organization with and on behalf of prisoners and their families. She is also a cofounding resident of Harriet Tubman House (an interfaith community dedicated to restorative practices in earth stewardship and human rights), has been a professor of philosophy, ethics, and religion, and has written essays for several books on theology and incarceration, including *And the Criminals with Him: Essays in Honor of Will D. Campbell and All the Reconciled.*

Onleilove Chika Alston is a preacher, writer and founder of the teaching ministry Prophetic Whirlwind: Uncovering the Black Biblical Destiny, which is dedicated to uncovering the African roots of the scripture and the true biblical identity of women. Born and raised in Brooklyn, Onleilove met Yahshua as a child facing homelessness and foster care, and this encounter with grace sustains her. Learn more about her work at www.PropheticWhirlwind.com.

Rose Marie Berger, author of *Bending the Arch: Poems* and *Who Killed Donte Manning?: The Story of an American Neighborhood*, is senior associate editor at *Sojourners* magazine, a Catholic peace activist, and a poet. She blogs at www.rosemarieberger. com.

Chris Broadwell is partner to Emily, parent to two children, and pastor to a United Methodist congregation in Annapolis, Maryland. He serves an intergenerational congregation that cares deeply for its neighbors.

Dana Cassell loves books, the Blue Ridge mountains, and her tiny dog named Franny. She is the pastor at Peace Covenant Church of the Brethren in Durham, North Carolina. She sometimes blogs at danacassell.wordpress.com.

Cat Caya resides with her husband, Jim, in southern California. She is learning and exploring at the intersection of spirituality, creativity, and justice and can be found on Instagram @catcaya.

Kayla Craig believes in the power of story, and with a background in journalism, she hopes to listen and learn from those on the margins, weave stories that cross divides, and sow love instead of hate. A co-host of *Upside Down Podcast*, Kayla lives in Iowa with her pastor-husband, Jonny, where they're raising four children via birth and adoption. Connect at kaylacraig.com and on Instagram @kayla_craig.

Kaitlin Curtice is a Native American Christian author and speaker, who writes and speaks on the intersection of identity and faith. She is the author of *Native: Identity, Belonging and Rediscovering God.*

Rev. Angela Denker is a former sportswriter turned Lutheran pastor, writer, speaker, wife and mom of two little boys based in Minneapolis, Minnesota. Denker is the author of *Red State Christians: Meet the Voters Who Elected Donald Trump* and blogs at agoodchristianwoman.blogspot.com, where she tries to share Jesus' love and refute the rumors about women, Christians, motherhood, and Jesus.

Brendan Blowers De León grew up between Idaho and Petionville, Haiti. He has lived and worked in Costa Rica for over six years, assisting ministries that use technology to train church leaders and reach out to youth in isolated and marginalized areas. Brendan and his wife, Emely, live in the cloud forests of Costa Rica as co-managers of the Quetzal Education Research Center, a biological field station dedicated to education and conservation.

Cory Driver is an ordained ELCA Deacon and adjunct professor teaching at the intersections of religion, ethnicity, gender and nationality. He earned his PhD in Jewish religious cultures from Emory University.

Elrena Evans is editor and content strategist for Evangelicals for Social Action, where she curates articles dedicated to the intersection of faith and social justice. She holds an MFA in creative writing from Penn State and is the author of a short story collection, *This Crowded Night: And Other Stories,* and co-author of the essay collection *Mama, PhD: Women Write About Motherhood and Academic Life.*

Shannon K. Evans is the author of *Embracing Weakness: The Unlikely Secret to Changing the World.* She lives in central Iowa with her husband Eric and five children.

Gary Francis is currently a youth coordinator who works with middle and high school students in Miami, Florida, during the week. On the weekend, he is a food tour guide with a company called Miami Food Tours, and at night, he is an aspiring author writing books that call people back to the heart of God the Father.

Patrice Gopo, a firm believer in the power of personal narratives to create pathways of connection and understanding in society, often writes about racial identity formation, race relations, immigration, and belonging. Her first book, a collection of personal essays entitled *All the Colors We Will See: Reflections on Barriers, Brokenness, and Finding Our Way*, was a Fall 2018 Barnes & Noble Discover Great New Writers selection. Visit www.patricegopo.com to learn more.

Josina Guess was born in Alabama, grew up in Washington, DC, spent over a decade in Philadelphia, and has put down roots on four acres in rural Georgia with her husband and their four children. She has written for *Fourth Genre*, *About Place Journal*, *The Christian Century*, *Sojourners*, *Crop Stories*, *Fight Evil with Poetry*, and *Wisdom of Communities: Sustainability in Community*, vol. 4, and is assistant editor for the *Bitter Southerner*, an online magazine that depicts the changing narrative of the South.

Tamara Gurley is a speaker, writer, teacher, and devotional blogger who dabbles in spoken word. She is a fierce follower of Jesus, advocate for justice and freedom, Urban Cohort seminarian, and spiller of words at lifespilledlikewater.org, where she creates curriculum, poetry, and devotionals that promote Bible literacy, reconciliation, community, and personal encouragement.

Rachel G. Hackenberg is an author, speaker, and ordained minister. Her book *Denial Is My Spiritual Practice (and Other Failures of Faith)*, co-authored with Martha Spong, searches for faith through life's trials.

Austen Hartke is the author of *Transforming: The Bible and the Lives of Transgender Christians*, and the director of Transmission Ministry Collective, an online community dedicated to the spiritual care and leadership of gender-expansive Christians. Find more about Austen and his work at www.austenhartke.com.

Delonte Harrod is an entrepreneur and journalist who lives in the Washington, DC metro area and writes at *The Intersection*, an online magazine that covers technology, religion, and politics. He also works part-time as the lead photographer at DHarrod Photography and can be found on Twitter @ delonteharrod.

Juan Carlos Huertas is a husband, father, spiritual director, and pastor. His commitment to egalitarian relationships, role and gender fluidity, and men's spirituality continues to inspire and convict him. Juan Carlos is married to Shannon, and they have three children. He muses at spiritstirrer.org.

Tony Huynh is currently a student at Multnomah Biblical Seminary in Portland, Oregon, where he is pursuing a Master of Arts in theological studies, focusing on politics, gender, and sexuality. Tony serves as a youth leader in the English ministry at the church where he grew up.

Aundi Kolber is a licensed therapist, author, and speaker who is passionate about helping people cultivate wholeness in their lives. She is the author of *Try Softer: A Fresh Approach to Move Us Out of Anxiety, Stress, and Survival Mode—and into a Life of Connection and Joy.*

Kenji Kuramitsu is a chaplain, clinical social worker, and fourth-generation Chicagoan. Find him online @afreshmind and kenjikuramitsu.com.

Britney Winn Lee is an author of books, the editor for Red Letter Christians, and a director of a nonprofit community arts program. She lives in Shreveport, Louisiana, with her creative husband and big-hearted son and can be found online @britneywinnlee.

Zhailon Levingston is a writer, director, performing artist, and activist. He cofounded #WORDSONWHITE, an arts and activism campaign, and is an artist-in-resident for Columbia Law School.

Tanya Marlow is the author of *Those Who Wait: Finding God in Disappointment, Doubt and Delay.* Her writing on disability and ME has been published by *The Guardian* and *The Spectator.* She campaigns with #MEAction Network, and her blog, regular newsletter, and free downloadable book can be found at TanyaMarlow.com.

D. L. Mayfield lives and writes on the outskirts of Portland, Oregon, where she teaches community-based ESOL (English for Speakers of Other Languages) and has lived and worked in primarily immigrant and refugee neighborhoods for fifteen years. She is the author of several books, most recently *The Myth of the American Dream: Reflections on Affluence, Autonomy, Safety and Power.*

Michael T. McRay works with stories, most often with Narrative 4, Tenx9 Nashville, and The Storytelling Leader. He's the author of multiple books, including the recent *I Am Not Your Enemy: Stories to Transform a Divided World.* Learn more by visiting www.michaelmcray.com and @michaeltmcray on Facebook, Instagram, and Twitter.

Rev. Michelle Mejia is an ordained elder in The United Methodist Church, serving in the Baltimore-Washington Conference in her fifth year as pastor of Eastport United Methodist Church in Annapolis, Maryland. Michelle and her husband, Daniel, also an ordained elder in The United Methodist Church, most recently find delight in their journey of parenting one curious and charming toddler, who has brought both more joy and more need of coffee to their lives than they ever imagined possible.

Osheta Moore is a speaker, podcaster, and the author of *Shalom Sistas: Living Wholeheartedly in a Brokenhearted World*. Although she's a proud Texan, Moore lives in and deeply loves St. Paul, Minnesota, where, in addition to planting a multiethnic church with her husband, Osheta is the outreach and teaching pastor at Woodland Hills.

Soldier turned peacemaker, **Diana Oestreich** heard God's call to love her enemies in the most unlikely place: on the battlefield of Iraq. Diana is an activist, veteran, sexual assault nurse, and the key relationship officer at Preemptive Love, a global relief organization working to end war.

Iyabo Onipede is an intercultural development consultant and race equity educator located in Atlanta, Georgia. She is a multicultural and multiracial global nomad, supporting institutions (higher education, nonprofits, businesses, governmental entities) as they create compassionate organizational cultures that reflect inclusion, equity, and justice in their processes, outputs, and leadership talent. Her online home is www.coachiyabo.com.

Elaina Ramsey serves as the executive director of the Ohio Religious Coalition for Reproductive Choice as well as the interim executive director of Red Letter Christians. A passionate community organizer and a former editor for Red Letter Christians and *Sojourners* magazine, Elaina loves listening to people's stories and engaging communities for social change.

Breanna Randall lives in southeast Asia with her husband and two daughters. More of her writing can be found at burmachronicle.com.

Bruce Reyes-Chow is one of the pastors at First Presbyterian Church of Palo Alto (CA), a senior coach with Convergence, host of the *BRC and Friends Podcast*, author of five books, husband to one amazing human, dad of three children, cuddler with the canines, sideline cheerer for the beautiful game, and still in process.

Dee Dee Risher is a writer and editor, worship leader, and activist. She is the author of *The Soulmaking Room*, a founder of Vine and Fig Tree (an intentional Christian cohousing community in Philadelphia), a cofounder of Philadelphia's Alternative Seminary, and a board member of Karitas.

Nikki Roberts is a justice-involved Black queer writer, public speaker, advocate, activist, and consultant who's studied both mass communications and theology on collegiate levels. Nikki's advocacy focuses on the independent and variously intersecting topics of race, gender, identity, criminal justice reform, trauma, healing-centered engagement, theology, and patterns of social relationships.

Brandan Robertson serves as the Lead Pastor of Missiongathering Christian Church in San Diego, California, and works as an instructor, consultant, and organizer with various national and international NGO's, religious denominations, and governmental organizations. Robertson is the author or contributing author to eight books, including *Our Witness: The Unheard Stories of LGBT+ Christians* and *The Gospel of Inclusion: A Christian Case for LGBT+ Inclusion in the Church.*

A New York native, **Sharifa Stevens** earned a bachelor of arts from Columbia University and a master of theology from Dallas Theological Seminary. She is wife to a Renaissance man and mother to two lively boys. Find her @sharifawrites or sharifastevens.com.

Sandra Maria Van Opstal is a pastor, activist, and liturgist consulting and training at the intersection of worship and justice. She pastors at Grace and Peace Church and is the author of *The Next Worship: Glorifying God in a Diverse World.* Find her at sandravanopstal.com.

Born in Venezuela, **AnaYelsi Velasco-Sanchez** is an IndoLatinx mujerista working to create and agitate her way through the Latin diaspora. With over a decade of nonprofit and faith-based community organizing experience, she now works independently—pursuing justice in an intersectional and holistic way as a consultant, educator, writer, and visual artist in both sacred and secular spaces.

Stephanie Vos is an artist, healer, and teacher. A mystic at heart, her work, either as a pastor or somatic therapist, has focused on the mystery of dimensionality, the interconnectedness of community, and reimagining our relationship with the natural world. Find more of her writing at TheSaltCollective.org.

Lindsy Wallace writes from Louisville, Kentucky, where she, her husband, and their five kids endeavor to love their neighbors as they love themselves. She is passionate about downward mobility, ushering in a more livable planet, and good tattoos and is co-host of *Upside Down Podcast*, an ecumenical conversation about faith, justice, and the upside-down kingdom of Jesus.

Erin F. Wasinger loves stories: she runs an elementary school library in Michigan, writes, and is creating a children's ministry curriculum called *Pray,*

Gather, Play: A Storytelling Method for God-Hungry Kids. Along with Sarah Arthur, Erin is also the coauthor of *The Year of Small Things: Radical Faith for the Rest of Us.*

Rev. Andrew Wilkes is a principal of Wilkes Advocacy Group, the co-lead pastor of the new church start The Double Love Experience in Brooklyn, New York, and the former associate pastor of Social Justice and Young Adults at the Greater Allen A.M.E. Cathedral of New York (GAC). A bi-vocational minister, Reverend Wilkes resides in Harlem with his wife, Min. Gabby Cudjoe-Wilkes and can be found on Twitter @AndrewJWilkes.

Jonathan Wilson-Hartgrove directs the School for Conversion (www.schoolforconversion.org) in Durham, North Carolina, and is the author of *Reconstructing the Gospel: Finding Freedom from Slaveholder Religion.*

Lydia Wylie-Kellermann is a writer, editor, and mother from Detroit, Michigan. She is the editor of *Geez magazine,* which seeks to hold space at the intersection of art, activism, and spirit.

NOTES

1. Thayer and Smith, "Greek Lexicon entry for *Leitourgia*," *The NAS New Testament Greek Lexicon*, 1999, https://www.biblestudytools.com/lexicons/greek/nas/leitourgia.html.
2. "Our tears cannot stop" is a phrase used to honor the African American academic and theologian Michael Eric Dyson and his book *Tears We Cannot Stop: A Sermon to White America* (New York: St. Martin's Press, 2017).
3. Narrative 4 is an organization that "equips people to use their stories to build empathy, shatter stereotypes, break down barriers, and—ultimately—make the world a better place." For more information, visit https://narrative4.com/about/.

Recommended by
The Academy
for spiritual Formation®
THE UPPER ROOM

For those who hunger for deep spiritual experience . . .

The Academy for Spiritual Formation® is an experience of disciplined Christian community emphasizing holistic spirituality—nurturing body, mind, and spirit. The program, a ministry of The Upper Room®, is ecumenical in nature and meant for all those who hunger for a deeper relationship with God, including both lay and clergy persons. Each Academy fosters spiritual rhythms—of study and prayer, silence and liturgy, solitude and relationship, rest and play.

With offerings of both Two-Year and Five-Day models, Academy participants rediscover Christianity's rich spiritual heritage through worship, learning, and fellowship. During the Two-Year Academy, pilgrims gather at a retreat center for five days every three months over the course of two years (a total of 40 days), and the Five-Day Academy is a modified version of the Two-Year experience, inviting pilgrims to gather for five days of spiritual leadership and worship. The Academy's commitment to an authentic spirituality promotes balance, inner and outer peace, holy living and justice living—God's shalom.

Faculty trained in the wide breadth of Christian spirituality and practice provide content and guidance at each session of The Academy. Academy faculty presenters come from seminaries, monasteries, spiritual direction ministries, and pastoral ministries or other settings and are from a variety of traditions.

The ACADEMY RECOMMENDS program seeks to highlight content that aligns with the Academy's mission to create transformative space for people to connect with God, self, others, and creation for the sake of the world.

Learn more by visiting academy.upperroom.org.